West

to

East

A Young Girl's Journey to China

Qian Gao

Edited by Erik Noyes and James J. Wang
Photos by Yanding Gao
Cover design by Linda Revel

Published in cooperation with Greatwall Books & Arts, Inc., 9114 Bellaire Blvd., Houston, Texas 70036.

First Edition, March 1996

Library of Congress Catalog Card Number: 95-83313
ISBN 0-8351-2549-1

Printed in Canada.

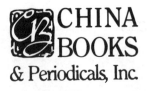

CHINA
BOOKS
& Periodicals, Inc.

Acknowledgements

My sincere thanks go to the people who have helped me make my book what it is. Without their help, this book would never have been possible.

These people include:

My parents, who loved me, supported me and encouraged me all along the way. From the very beginning, when West to East was only a journal to its present book form, their love, support and encouragement have not dimmed the least bit.

All my friends and my parent's friends who encouraged me to keep on going after they read my manuscript or portions of it. In fact, they did not stop at encouragement, but they also made a lot of constructive suggestions. I owe these people my deep gratitude.

Staff of China Books & Periodicals.

My friends in China, including Helen Cheng and Sophia Wong in Hong Kong, Xu Hong (Xu Laolao) in Beijing, and all my relatives in Fuzhou, especially my grandmother (Nai-nai).

Thank you all for making my dream come true.

Author's Note

My name "Qian" is pronounced "Chin".

When I use names of people living in China, the family name comes first since this is the order in which they are normally used in China.

Most of the Chinese names and places have been transliterated into the standard pinyin system, unless in cases of well-known names or places like Hong Kong (Xiang Gang) and the Yangtze River (Chang Jiang).

When I refer to some people in my family, I use their titles rather than their names. For example, instead of using my grandmothers' real names, I call them Nai-nai (Grandma-paternal) and Wai-po (Grandma-maternal).

To Mommy & Daddy
for their love

Preface

I was born in China in 1981, and came to the United States when I was five years old. As I slowly started learning English, I also started reading books. I realized that reading was fun.

My parents had a lot to do with my love for reading. Each time I finished a new book, I would show it to my parents, and they would compliment me. Every child likes compliments and I was no exception.

The library started feeling like a second home to me. The librarians started to recognize me when I came in for another book.

During all those years, I gave very little thought to how the books were written. I gave no thought to the authors. To me, authors were just a name on the book cover.

I thought that writing a book must be extremely easy since so many books came out each year. My reasoning was that if it was so hard, then why were there so many books in a library?

In the fifth grade, I started to realize that I was wrong; authors have a difficult job. That was the year we actually started writing lengthy reports and creative papers. The hours of thinking and writing about one topic were enough, let alone the hours of editing and revising. My papers were just a few pages long, yet books were often two hundred pages or more. If it took me that long just to finish a paper, how long did it take authors to write a whole book? It didn't take me long to find out.

Our trip to China in December 1992 was one of the most exciting events of my life. I felt that I should document it for a keepsake. Before we left for China, I promised that I would try my best to write every day in my journal.

As we sped through the towns, I realized very quickly that my objective would be impossible. I found that our schedule usually started at eight in the morning and ended at midnight. Since there was no time to keep a complete journal, I decided to write brief notes about what we did each day, leaving the task of filling in the details when I got back to Texas.

Throughout the trip, I noticed many differences between western and eastern life. The food was different and the clothes were different but most of all, there was a huge cultural difference. Since I had grown up in the United States, my parents often said that my way of thinking was very "Westernized."

When I first got to China, the culture shock was one of my major problems. The way Chinese people did things was strange to me and many of their customs seemed foolish. However, as I stayed there longer and grew accustomed to the culture, I began to find similarities.

During my stay in Fuzhou, I started to look upon my journal as a book. I wanted to share my adventures with other people. What could be better than sharing what I had learned? Perhaps I could foster some understanding, on a small scale of course, among the people of both cultures.

When I got back to the United States, I sat down to write my book. It was a lot harder than I had imagined it would be.

In December1993, I finally completed the entire manuscript. It had taken me nearly a year to get it done.

This book is a chronicle of the things I saw and felt. My objective in writing this book is to tell people what a person with my background thinks of China. This is my objective and I hope I have succeeded in it.

BEIJING
★

The People's Republic of China

● SHANGHAI

●J FUZHOU

GUANGZHOU
●
●
HONG KONG

November 29, 1992

Oh, the pain, the excitement, the fear, the sorrow! How can these emotions hit someone so hard? How can they speed in and distort one's life so much as it does me? Well, I am learning that they can because I am feeling these emotions all at the same time. I have longed to visit China and ever since we decided to go, I have been counting the days until we get on the airplane. Today is the last one on the calendar and I cannot wait!

I was leaving the next day and these emotions washed over me. I didn't want to leave my friends and home, yet I also had a powerful need to go. I felt excited because this trip would take me almost around the whole world. I felt scared because I might get lost in China. I mean China has the largest population in the world with a billion people. If I could manage to get lost in New York City, which I did, I would probably get lost in China. Sorrow was an emotion any other kid my age would have felt because I was leaving everything behind.

I was born in China, and I came to Texas when I was five years old. My father works at the Texas A&M University. He brought our family here in 1986. I remember when I first came here, I was just a little thing who couldn't speak English at all. I have been here for six years now so I have lived longer in the United States than in China. Even so, I consider China my first home.

It was very hard for me to remember all my relatives and my life in China six years before. I didn't have any special friends there and I hardly remembered anyone. The only relative I remembered well was my grandmother. We have a special relationship that no one could ever break. We can read each other's mind sometimes and I can talk to her without feeling awkward.

She had come to visit us in November 1991 and went back to China in January, just in time to face heartache: a few short days after her return, my grandfather fell down some stairs and hit his head. He suffered a stroke and fell into a coma.

My grandfather never came out of his coma but he was strong until the end. He lived seven more months before he passed away. One day in late August, we received a fax that he had died the day before. He is now buried in Xichan Temple in Fuzhou.

We had planned on going to China before my grandfather died. My parents wanted to go back to see all their relatives and close friends. My dad also wanted me to visit China. He said that since I was Chinese, I should know more about my own country.

The fax we received about my grandfather's death made it more necessary to go. My grandmother needed us and we weren't about to disappoint her.

We would fly to Hong Kong. There, we would stay for two or three days. Then, we planned on visiting Guangzhou. Where next? The capital, Beijing, where we would visit the ancient Forbidden City and the many beautiful parks. I had read about them so I knew where each park was. I made my dad a bit crazy because I would keep telling him where we absolutely had to go, which was everywhere. After Beijing, we were to take a train to Shanghai, the largest city in China. Last but certainly not least, we would see the wonderful city of Fuzhou, where I was born. We would stay there for two weeks and visit friends and relatives and then head on back.

We would visit Hong Kong again for a short period of time on our way back. Then, we would finally arrive back at College Station on January 5th. What a whirlwind! And it was only a day away.

November 30, 1992

Someone was holding me by the shoulders and shaking my brains out. I opened my eyes to see my mother. I ignored her and soon I was fast asleep again. Not for long, though. This time she pulled me up and forced me to get up.

All of a sudden my eyes were open and they flew to the clock. I let out a yell and jumped out of bed. In less than thirty seconds, I was changing clothes. We were leaving at six o'clock and it was already five fifteen.

My mom was cooking noodles and my dad was busy putting his computer in a box. He had bought two laser printers, a computer and a monitor that he was planning to sell in China.

After a quick breakfast of noodles, we were ready to leave. We loaded the suitcases and electronics into the trunk and squeezed into the car. As we left the driveway, my eyes were glued to my home until it was out of sight. I silently said good-bye to College Station and all my friends one by one. As we drove onto the highway, my thoughts shifted to the places we would be visiting. I couldn't wait. My grandmother obviously couldn't either. She was upset that we wouldn't go to Fuzhou first.

I wanted to jump up and down. I couldn't wait to get to China but I didn't want to leave College Station either because I would miss my friends so much.

I was still deep in thought when Mr. Li, my father's friend, exclaimed, "We're at the airport!" The Houston Intercontinental Airport was extremely large but I wasn't impressed. Who would be with what I had ahead of me?

December 1, 1992
December 2, 1992

I have always wanted to go to Hong Kong. It sounds so al-
luring and special. I can't wait to get there. I don't feel like
sitting still. I want to jump up and down. I want the whole
world to know where I will be in a few short hours.

I practically did laps around the plane for the last two
hours of our flight. When I got back to my seat, my mom
and dad were talking about Ms. Cheng, whose American
name is Helen. Helen used to work with my dad in a machine and tools company in Fuzhou. She used to live there
but now she lived with her daughter Sophia, in Hong Kong.
My dad and Helen were good friends so when she found out
that we were coming to Hong Kong, she offered her apartment to us.

Toward the end of our flight, an attendant came down the
aisle selling duty-free items such as cigarettes, perfume and
watches. The prices were reasonable so we looked through
their brochure.

We finally decided to buy a few things. Since cigarettes
were popular presents in China, my dad bought as many as
he could fit into his carry-on bag. We also bought four bottles
of French perfume, planning to give Sophia one of them.

Suddenly, I could feel the plane tip forward. I looked out
the window and I could see islands and trees. The little cars
driving on the highways were so tiny I had to squint to see
them.

Finally, the plane dove down sharply. I thought we were
going to crash so I put my hand under my seat. I was ready
to pull out the emergency suit. In a matter of seconds, we
were on the ground so I quickly removed my hand. I felt
silly with my hand under my seat.

We disembarked at the Kai Tak Airport in Kowloon, where we were going to take a taxi to the famous city, Hong Kong.

Hong Kong is still a British colony until 1997. It lies at the mouth of the Pearl River delta which is just a little north of Macau. Hong Kong consists of Hong Kong Island and an archipelago of some 230 smaller islands, which are mostly uninhabited. Kowloon, where we landed, is near Hong Kong but is considered on the Chinese mainland.

After going through customs, we found the baggage claim. Since we had so many suitcases, we had to use two carts to carry everything.

We finished changing money and pushed our carts to the meeting place where, sure enough, Helen was waiting for us. Since this was the first time I had ever seen her, I was extremely surprised. She was nowhere near the picture I had made of her in my mind.

She turned out to be a very talkative person, so I guess that was part of the reason she and I got along so well. We all walked out of the building and headed for the taxi stand.

We got two taxis, but it was still hard to fit everything in. After much huffing and puffing, we finally managed.

Helen and I climbed in the first taxi while my parents situated themselves in the second. While Helen and the taxi driver babbled on and on about the weather and news, I tried to enjoy the sights about me.

The only things that were distracting to me were all the cars honking horns. In Texas, people hardly ever honk their horns, but here they seemed to honk just for the fun of it. It never ended. The huge traffic jam further shocked me. I can not remember ever seeing anything like this. The streets were so packed with cars they looked like parking lots. Even when there were parades in Texas, there weren't this many cars.

As soon as we got into Hong Kong I saw a change. I guess you could say Hong Kong had a more sophisticated air than

Kowloon. Also, there wasn't so much noise and filth.

Soon, we stopped in front of some very impressive-looking buildings. Helen got out of the car and ran into the building to get the superintendent to open the gate. The taxi drivers helped us unload all the stuff, and with everything finally inside her apartment, I sat down in a chair to rest. Suddenly, a dog jumped out at me from nowhere. I was extremely surprised and nearly fell out of the chair. This animal Bobo and I soon became good friends.

When we finally settled down in Helen's apartment, my parents and Helen sat down and started talking. They ignored everything else as they talked and talked. I knew they were enjoying themselves. A warmness spread through me. I could just imagine not seeing my friends for 15 years and then suddenly being given the opportunity to see and talk to them again. I would savor each moment as they were.

The sun shone in on all of the rooms. Everything took on a cheerful glow.

Soon, we were talking about Sophia. Since Helen wanted her daughter to come to the United States to study and live with us, my dad had brought some brochures from a private school. They started poring over them.

While we were all seated around the table, talking about Sophia, I heard a key turning in the lock. I knew it was Sophia and I couldn't wait to meet her since Helen had listed all the similarities between the two of us.

Sophia came bursting in the room. When I saw her, I found she was exactly as I had imagined.

I found out everything I needed to know in the next half hour. Sophia was fifteen years old and she was nice and sincere. We were immediately good friends.

Sophia had a tutor coming over soon, so the rest of us decided to go out and take in the sights and sounds of Hong Kong.

Before long we were out in the streets. Our first stop was a supermarket. We looked at the food and compared the prices with those in the U.S. Most of the food was much more expensive. The price of certain fruit was absolutely outrageous.

We left the supermarket and walked into the mall. I couldn't believe the size of it. It was much larger than our mall at home. We walked around and windowshopped for a while. Finally Sophia joined us. Since she was hungry, I agreed to accompany her to McDonald's. This was the first time I had ever been in a McDonald's outside of the U.S., so I was pretty curious to see what it would be like.

To my surprise, it was exactly like any McDonald's in the U.S. The only difference was the menu. It was in both English and Chinese.

After lunch we reacquired our parents and strolled slowly down the arcade of shops. Every one of us seemed ready to collapse so nobody said much. I knew I was jet lagged because as soon as I walked in the door to Helen's apartment, I collapsed on my guest bed and fell asleep the minute my head touched the pillow.

December 3, 1992

Something is barking in my ear and licking my face.

I jumped up and found that it was Bobo. I picked him up and put him on the floor. There was nobody else in the room so I hopped out of bed and headed for the living room. My mom was sitting at the dining table and Helen was in the kitchen. My dad was still lying in his little sleeping bag on the floor.

Soon, everybody was assembled around the dining table except Sophia who had already left for school. During breakfast, dad told us that we had been invited to dinner by his former teacher. My dad had worked at the Fujian Institute of Research on the Structure of Matter, Chinese Academy of Sciences before he came to the U.S., and his teacher was vice director.

Mr. Liu now lived in Hong Kong but his wife still worked in Fuzhou. When he heard my dad would be in Hong Kong for three days, he immediately invited us to dinner. Although our days in Hong Kong were already very tight, my dad accepted his invitation.

After breakfast, we set off for an outdoors market called North Point Market. It was in another part of the city so we had to take the subway. The cold air whisked around us. I wrapped my jacket around me tightly. I wasn't used to this piercing wind and freezing cold. We entered the mall we were in the day before and then went down into the subway station right below it.

We all got on the subway and stood with the crowd of people because there were no free seats. In fact, there were hardly any free standing spots.

Coming out of the station, I step onto a noisy street. I can't believe what meets my eyes. Right there in front of me is the market. I have never dreamed of anything like this, especially after seeing Helen's apartment and the environment in which she lives.

The difference is incredible. People are crowded around in the streets. Boxes and little push carts are right at home amid the commotion on the street. Only the stores that sell formal and business clothing have awnings but even these are just shabby ceilings. I doubt that they are effective in keeping out the wind and the cold.

Little bits of paper and trash are strewn everywhere. It is horrible that people just litter in full view of everyone else. They don't seem to think twice about it. I can tell I still have a lot to learn about Hong Kong.

We walked down the street, inspecting each shop's and sidewalk vendor's wares. My dad was interested in buying some shirts and my mom and I were looking for dresses.

Helen was a great help. Since almost everybody in Hong Kong spoke Cantonese and nobody in our family understood it, Helen became our translator. I quickly learned from Helen that if the people selling the products heard you speaking Mandarin, they would assume you were from China. They would then try to rip you off. If you were from a country like the U.S., they would probably sell it to you for three or four times the real price.

My dad stopped suddenly in front of some carts. Shirts! They were only twenty five Hong Kong dollars. Talk about cheap.

The man selling the shirts noticed that we were speaking Chinese. He immediately struck up a conversation with us.

"Where are you from?" he asked. "I can tell you're not Cantonese. Are you from China?"

Before we could answer, he announced, "I'm from Harbin." The man seemed to think that it was time to tell us his life story. "I've been selling shirts on this street for ten years now. I have an uncle who owns a clothing factory in Hong Kong. Ten years ago, I decided to come to Hong Kong to work for him. I had no idea about businessmen like him - someone so completely devoid of compassion. He acted like he didn't know me because I was poor.

"Well," he pulled at his own lapel, "he was considerate enough to give me a job in his factory with a very low salary. After a few months, I told him I wanted to sell shirts, so I bought some from him and came here to sell them."

After a brief pause, he continued, "You see all these people selling things here?"

We nodded.

"Every one of them has bought protection from the gangsters who run this area."

I though this man must have been out in the cold for too long. Did he mean what he said? How can you buy protection? Anyway, who would trust gangsters with their safety?

"Every person here has been accosted by gang members. The gang members force them to pay money. In return, they get protection. Well, on my second day here, two men came up to me and demanded that I pay my protection fee. I flatly refused. As is the gangster's custom, they tried to beat me up for refusing to pay. The gangster threw the first blow," he related with a smile.

At this point of the story, he was starting to get worked up.

"I had taken martial arts classes since I was four years old. Well, by the time I was done, those two gangsters were rolling around on the ground."

I smiled when he got to this part. To me, he didn't look tough. He did look pretty shady but he was too skinny to look tough.

"The next day, the gang leader and a few others came to visit me. At the end of the visit, I was nonchalantly choking their leader. The other members were staring at me with their mouths wide open. When I let go of the leader, his fighting spirit had already left him. He looked at me with newfound respect and asked me to join the gang. Now I'm part of the gang but I'm not really part of it. We settled for a kind of

truce. The other gang members don't bother me about protection fees and I don't go with them to collect their fees
from the others," he grinned.

My dad asked, "Well, how much do you earn per day?"

"You see these shirts here? They're top quality. In the
fancy stores, they sell these for sixty *gangbi* (Hong Kong
dollars). Here, I sell them for twenty five. I earn ten *gangbi*
for every shirt because I pay my uncle fifteen *gangbi* per
shirt, and I usually sell two hundred shirts a day without any
problem." he estimated.

"That's two thousand *gangbi* a day?" my dad sputtered.

That would be around three hundred U.S. dollars.

"That's right!" he said proudly.

"Is it so easy to earn money in Hong Kong?" my dad
asked, incredulous.

"No way! Only if you have the right connections. For
example, not everybody has an uncle like mine. Since I'm
kin, he lets me choose the shirts I want. Naturally, I choose
the best ones. He also sells the shirts to me a little cheaper.
And don't overlook the necessity for self-defense. Those protection fees can be extremely high."

After a few seconds, he started boasting.

"I had a bride imported from China just last year. Pretty
as a porcelain doll. I bought a *lou* last year, too."

Lou means building so I was really impressed.

"How big is your *lou*?" my dad asked.

"One bedroom, one living room, one bathroom and one
kitchen," he announced proudly.

It was obvious that building to him meant an apartment.

Then, he asked us where we were from again. When my
dad said the United States, he didn't seem surprised.

He just said, "Twenty five *gangbi* is pretty cheap for you,
isn't it?

My dad just nodded.

"If they don't fit you, you can bring them back tomorrow
and exchange them," he said.

My dad thanked the man and we left his cart. By this

time, our stomachs were all growling and my legs were so tired they might as well have been paralyzed. Helen noticed and led us into a huge building. We took an escalator to the top floor.

There were three or four restaurants but they didn't have walls separating them. They didn't have names, either. Instead of chairs, they used stools. We could also see the chefs cooking because they didn't have kitchens. The chefs just cooked away in a little corner. Every restaurant had two or three people working in it.

We picked a restaurant and sat down to eat. I didn't like the stools at all because I couldn't lean back. Helen needed to use the restroom so I went with her. I noticed she brought along a bag of Kleenexes.

Even before we got to the restroom, I smelled a foul odor. When we entered it, I knew immediately where the odor had been coming from.

Before I entered a stall, Helen passed me a few Kleenexes. There was no tissue paper in the restrooms. I also learned that no restrooms in Hong Kong or China, except those in big hotels, would provide tissue paper.

When I entered the stall, I got another surprise. There was no toilet! Just a hole in the ground! By this time, I had had enough of these surprises. How in the world was I supposed to use a restroom with a hole in the ground and no toilet?

Finally, I realized that I was supposed to bend down to use it. After I finished, I didn't know how to flush it. I heard Helen flush so I knew there had to be some kind of switch somewhere. That was when I saw the rope above me.

I hurriedly left the restroom with Helen and we found our table. My mom and dad were talking so I didn't bother them with my newfound restroom discoveries.

Pretty soon, the cashier/waiter came over and took our orders. We had all kinds of seafood and meats. It tasted much better and it was much cheaper than the Chinese food in the

U.S.

After our meal, we paid our bill. It was too bad there was no fortune cookie but I wasn't expecting one. My dad had told me that fortune cookies didn't start in China but in the U.S.

We were meeting my dad's friend, Mr. Liu for dinner so we took the subway to meet him. When we emerged at the proper subway stop, we saw a whole different side of Hong Kong. The street lights were brightly lit and everyone was wearing bright-colored clothing. Hong Kong seemed to be made up of three distinct worlds. It had a First World, a Third World and a Middle World. We were definitely in the First World now.

When we walked into the Seafood Palace restaurant, Mr. Liu wasn't there. We sat down at a table and waited for him. Within a few minutes, he arrived and introduced himself.

He did most of the ordering since we weren't very sure what to order. The first thing that came was the lobster. Staring at it made my mouth water but I waited until someone else took the first portion.

Pretty soon, our table had all kinds of seafood on it. We had had seafood for lunch but it seemed very different from dinner. They were both delicious but the food at lunchtime seemed more enjoyable because I wasn't afraid of gorging myself.

After dinner, Mr. Liu took us around the shops. Then, he gave us a ride in his car to the subway station. Having a car in Hong Kong is expensive, and not only for the cars but also for the parking spaces. Renting a parking space for a month could cost up to four hundred U.S. dollars.

December 4, 1992

Today should be a day of wonders, I thought to myself as I opened my eyes. I jumped out of bed and immediately realized that Sophia was still in bed and she was snoring like a chainsaw.

After everybody was up, we had breakfast. Helen showed us the train tickets to Guangzhou her friend had gotten for us. We were very grateful and thanked her profusely. We probably couldn't have gotten train tickets ourselves on such short notice.

Sophia and I voted to go to the Pacific Place, which is a mall in Hong Kong that was supposed to be enormously expensive. As usual, our parents outvoted us. We had to go to North Point Market again by subway.

To my surprise, the subway wasn't as crowded and I even got a seat. We didn't stay lucky. At the next stop, millions of people rushed in. You had to squeeze really hard just to get out.

After I stepped out of the subway station, we were engulfed by the crowd. Since my dad only needed to change the shirts he bought the day before, we didn't need to spend too much time there. The man remembered us and he let my dad pick out some bigger shirts.

My eyes started to wander. Soon, they moved to a little cart. The shirt on it was really unusual. I rushed over and picked it up. It had a picture of a Chinese flag over the British flag with the words "Hong Kong" over "1997". I immediately decided to buy a few of these T-shirts for my friends. We didn't stay here for a long time because our train for Guangzhou was scheduled to depart at two o'clock. The clock read twelve-thirty.

The ride to Kowloon's train station wasn't very comfortable and to make matters worse, the traffic was horrendous. My mom noticed a man on a bicycle at the side of the road. She started talking about how long it had been since she had ridden a bicycle. Sophia smiled. "Don't worry. This is only Hong Kong. You're about to enter bicycle heaven," she warned jokingly.

The two taxis stopped right in front of the station. There were many men and women standing outside. The minute we got out of the taxis, two women came rushing over. At first, I thought they were going to try to steal something but they didn't. My mom talked to them. They ended up following us to the check-in counter but they never got too close.

When we sat down in the waiting area, the two women came over again. We found out they wanted us to sell them one of our laser printers and take it to Guangzhou for them. We refused many times but they just wouldn't give up.

Sophia and I dreamed up many ways to make them leave but no matter what we did, they wouldn't leave. Since this was illegal, Sophia and I didn't want our parents to get involved.

I have to admit the women were extremely polite but I was sure they had done this a million times. After a while, they realized they were going to get nowhere with us and they stormed away angrily.

After they left, we lined up to board the train. We said all our tearful goodbyes. As the train pulled away, I waved one last time to Sophia and Helen and then they disappeared as we rounded a bend.

You notice the difference between Hong Kong and China the minute you get on the train to China. The train is filthy and crowded. The only good point is that we are seated in the soft seat section which is pretty comfortable.

Soon, a man wearing a suit came over. He put his hand on the top of the seat and looked down at us with a strange smile on his face. He heard us speaking Fuzhou dialect and asked

"Where are you from?"

"The United States, Texas," my dad answered.

"Oh really? I'm from New York." My dad didn't answer, so he continued proudly, "I went to the U.S. as an illegal immigrant."

I didn't understand why he was so proud of something like that. He seemed to be looking for something to talk about, so he told us about his fake marriage. He must have seen that we weren't very interested in his life story, because he turned his attention to us next.

"Do you really live in the United States?" he asked. For some reason, he was suspicious. "Do you work in a restaurant?" he asked my dad.

My dad turned red but he answered, "No, I work at a university."

"Oh!" he exclaimed. "Do you teach?"

"No, I'm an instrument specialist in the chemistry department," my dad told him. "What do you do for a living?"

"Actually, I work in a restaurant."

He looked me over and then said wickedly, "You're making us overseas Chinese look bad. The whole point of coming back for a visit is to make a good impression. You could at least dress right."

I looked at his choice of clothes. He had on an expensive-looking suit and very pungent cologne. His fingers were covered with rings including a large, ruby pinky ring. It was so huge I doubted it was meant to be a pinky ring. He kept on flashing it in our face as if it was something precious we could never have.

"Don't you understand? You have to dress well..."

I kept dozing off and waking up every ten minutes, only to find he was still talking. Finally, the speaker came on telling us we were about to enter Guangzhou.

What a sight! The ground looks as if it has been overcome by litter. The platform smells like a toilet. All kinds of people are swarming around in packs. Everything and ev-

erybody is in an utterly confused state.

The sky is gray and hazy from pollution. Cars go zooming past. People are all over the streets. Everything seems so disgusting, different and dangerous. I want to go straight back to Hong Kong.

As I stood rooted to the ground with shock, my dad left to find a phone. He needed to find a hotel for us.

My mom and I waited outside the train station for an hour and a half. When he returned, he had found a hotel called Liuhua Hotel. It was just across the street from the train station. It was very expensive in the Chinese sense but we decided to stay there anyway. When we finally found a taxi, we had a hard time fitting all our stuff in it. I was extremely glad the hotel wasn't far off.

Usually in hotels all over the United States, the bellboy is supposed to help you carry your suitcases. Well, that bellboy just stood there grinning at us like a stupid monkey, so we had to struggle with our own suitcases unaided.

When we had finally managed to get all the luggage into the hotel, we got a room on the seventh floor at the front desk. While my parents were paying, I had noticed the girl sitting behind the counter acting like she was Miss Universe and we were just dust on the point of her shoe. She had hardly even glanced at us.

We found the room; it was just a regular double-bed bedroom, but to me it was much more than that. It was a place I could lie down and rest. I was asleep even before my eyes were closed.

December 5, 1992

The sunlight streams through the window. This is our first day in Guangzhou!

We had to go to the train station to pick up our laser printer as instructed by the customs officials. When we walked out of the hotel the sky was filled with pollution that was so gray it almost looked like a huge raincloud. I couldn't believe people survived in Guangzhou with all the bad air.

After looking around, I recognized a health hazard much worse than air pollution. There were no lanes on the road so cars were just zooming around out of control! How in the world was I going to cross the street to the train station?

I had to hold hands with my parents while crossing the street because if I had tried to cross the street by myself, I would have been applesauce in no time.

When we got to the train station, everything was a mess. There were sleeping bags on the ground and people lying in them. They wore tattered clothes and their sleeping bags were so badly soiled they looked like they had just been washed in a mud puddle. Others roamed around begging for food and money.

After squinting several eternities at my dad's passport, the customs officers let my dad in while we were made to wait outside.

While outside, we looked around and I noticed a few children around the age of eight or nine in tattered clothing with tear and dirt-streaked faces begging for money and food. Whenever a taxi pulled up, the kids would all rush over and open the door. They would help the passengers with their luggage. Some people were nice and gave them money. If they didn't, the kids would hold on to their clothes and pull and beg and cry.

Whenever foreigners would get out of a car, adults would

come running also. I saw two mothers with their babies begging. The babies were screaming their heads off.

I thought it was weird that a baby would cry so incessantly so I took a closer look. When the next foreigner got out of her car, the mothers would run up to the car. Then, they would pinch their babies, causing them to wail even louder.

I was shocked. How could they do such a horrible thing to their own children? Money and food are important but I couldn't believe a mother would actually bring herself to pinch her baby. Then again, what do I know about near-starvation?

My dad finally came back with the laser printer and brought it up to our hotel room. I was starting to get hungry so we went out to find a restaurant. First, we walked into an extremely fancy restaurant. The first thing I saw was a dog hanging from the ceiling. Before my parents could even enter, I ran out. How could anybody actually eat a dog?

A few blocks down was a little restaurant we found. Outside, there was a huge glass jar full of snakes. The snakes were all slithering around. The sight of all those snakes was amusing until my dad informed me that we were having them for lunch.

I almost threw up right then and there.

When the food came to our table, I couldn't believe how delicious the snakes were. I tried not to think about their form during life.

After our lunch, we bought some nectarines and headed back for the hotel. Along the way, a few people came up to us and muttered under their breaths, "Wanta change Hong Kong dollars for U.S.?" or " Wanta change Chinese dollars for U.S.?"

The only reason anyone would actually change with them would be that the actual exchange rate the government set was 1 U.S. dollar equals around 5.8 Chinese dollars. These people would trade 7.1 or higher Chinese dollars for just 1

U.S. dollar. After they made the exchange, they would then sell the currency to someone else for a profit.

My dad decided to change some money but he wisely said that he wouldn't take out his money until the other man had handed the Chinese dollars over. We were trading at 1 U.S. dollar for 7.3 Chinese dollars. The man left to get some money and we waited for him to come back. He counted his own money in front of us and then handed it to my dad.

My dad said, "Wait, let me count again."

Right when he said this, the other guy said, "Fine, if you don't want to change..." He grabbed his money and stalked off.

I had noticed that after the man counted his own money, he had taken the two bottom bills and quickly stuffed them into his pocket. That was why he had left when my dad wanted to count it again.

When I told my parents this, I found out my dad had already noticed. Both of us had been wide awake.

We entered the hotel and went back to our room. By this time, I was so sleepy, my eyelids closed on their own accord.

December 6, 1992

What a morning! As was the other day and night, the sky is once again filled with pollution. It looks like the sun has just set even though it is early morning. Scientists say that the sun reaches every little point of the earth but I have found that to be false. The sun never seems to shine on Guangzhou.

We went into a restaurant for breakfast. In Guangzhou, the morning meal is a very important one so they have huge breakfasts. Their way of serving breakfast is very strange, though.

A waitress led us to a table and gave each one of us a little piece of paper that had numbers from one to fifty. Then she served tea.

The rest was up to us since the breakfast was kind of buffet style. Each food had a corresponding number which the waitresses would circle when you picked a dish. At the end of your breakfast, you would have to pay for all the numbers she had circled. By the time I had finished, I could hardly stand up, I was so full. My ticket was almost completely filled with circles.

After breakfast, we went back to our room and called my aunt. She was there and my dad found out the address to my grandmother's apartment. We were going to ship all of our large computer equipment to Fuzhou. Then, we got all the boxes and took them outside. We found a taxi and took off for the airport.

Finally, we had gone through the process of sending our boxes. It took us three hours because of the huge throng of people. We got out of the Baiyun Airport as fast as we could. By that time, we were all ready for a bit of fun.

We took a taxi to the Huanghuagang, or Yellow Flower Hill. Yellow Flower Hill was a park and a cemetery for the seventy-two people who incited a Revolution to do away with the dynastic system. The emperor ordered their murders. Later, this park was built in their honor.

After spending some time at this beautiful park, we took a taxi to Yuexiu Park. My dad wanted to show me the statue called Five Rams. Once we entered, it took us quite a while to find the actual statue because it was very well hidden. It was a statue of five rams eating grass. Five Rams is the nickname of Guangzhou and so this statue represented Guangzhou.

The scenery from the Five Rams was spectacular. Since it was so high up, you could look around and see the treetops and the surrounding wilderness. The only sights that saddened me were little specks of black soot on the leaves of the surrounding foilage. The polluted air was becoming maddening.

The pollution in Guangzhou is going to ruin Guangzhou's nature and wilderness.

After leaving the park, we took a taxi back to the hotel but we told the taxi driver to drive past the Zhu Jiang or Pearl River on the way. My dad wanted to show it to me.

When the taxi driver heard our request, he just snorted. He decided to express his opinion, "Who would want to see the river these days? There's nothing special about it. It's just oily and smelly water."

He took us there anyway and it looked just as I imagined it would. It was black, oily and polluted. We drove along the coast and looked at it but I was tired and I didn't feel like expressing my thoughts.

December 7, 1992

Our last morning in Guangzhou was hectic. Right after we got up, we took our backpack with all the books I had purchased the night before and walked out of the hotel. The minute we stepped out, a whole group of people came over to us and asked us to change money but we really didn't need to or want to. My dad got rid of them by taking out our camera.

"Smile!" my dad yelled.

Every one of them turned around and hurried off.

We took a taxi back to the center of the town. The taxi driver let us off before our destination because there had been an accident ahead.

My dad and I walked up close to it. My mom didn't come because she didn't want to get anywhere near the blood on the ground. There was a crowd of onlookers. A motorcycle had crashed head-on into a taxi and the driver of the motorcycle had died instantly. The blood on the ground was being swept away. I couldn't look at the blood any longer so we left.

We took another taxi to the Sun Yat-sen Memorial. My dad insisted that we go to the Sun Yat-sen Memorial since it was one of the most important places in Guangzhou.

Sun Yat-sen was a man of great honor in China. He was also known as Sun Wen and Sun Zhong Shan. He lived from 1866-1925. His college degree had been in medicine, but he soon realized that wouldn't help better his country. He gave up his job and founded the party which eventually became the Kuomintang Party in 1911. He led it to overthrow the Qing dynasty.

After overthrowing the dynasty, he became the president of the new republic but another man by the name of Yuan Shih-kai forced Sun Yat-sen out of his seat a month after his presidency began. Sun was enraged by the new president's policies. After leading an unsuccessful revolt in 1913, he fled to Japan.

In 1917, after the death of Yuan Shih-kai, Sun led the Kuomintang in establishing a Republic of South China in Guangzhou, Guangdong Province. He was president for a short period in 1918 and again in 1921 and 1922. From 1923 to his death, he was recognized as the chief executive of the Guangdong Province but his authority was confined to Guangzhou. Presently, he is most recognized for overthrowing the Qing dynasty and getting rid of the hateful braids from the old monarchy.

We took some pictures outside of the Memorial, then paid to go in. I was astounded by what met my eyes. The Memorial was beautiful. There were little rows of flowers on the sides and flowers in the middle of the wide walkway. There were bluebells, daisies, narcissuses and about every other kind of flower there is. It all seemed to come straight out of a storybook setting.

Behind all the rows of flowers was the Sun Yat-sen statue. It was the size of any other statue but what made it so special was whom it stood for.

My dad took out his camera. He started taking pictures of us but he was incredibly slow. He had to check every setting before clicking the button. It took him decades just to take one simple, little picture – hopeless.

We strolled around the park and looked at the scenery. However, it was getting close to eleven, and we had to go back to pack before our afternoon flight to Beijing.

As was the day before, we went to Baiyun Airport. We had to leave at around twelve-thirty because it would take twenty minutes just to drive there without any traffic jams. We had been in China long enough to know that there are always traffic jams.

Our taxi driver was very talkative. He talked a lot about

how China had changed, in his view, for the worse in the past few years but he mostly talked about Guangzhou.

In his slightly nasal tone, he said, "China is very different from what it used to be. Look at Guangzhou. A couple of years ago, it was just a plain old city. Maybe a little busier than others but now it's become a city of tourists instead of Chinese people.

"Too much crime nowadays, too. With all your luggage, you ought to be careful. Once I had a passenger that had a big screen TV. The lid of the rear trunk was also open like now, but I didn't think it would matter. When we got to his destination, the TV was gone. With all your luggage, you'd better look back whenever I stop."

So, there I was, with a crick in my neck from looking back. The fact that he stopped very often because of the traffic didn't help. My mom joined me in Operation Look Back.

When the car stopped at the front of the airport, I was the first one to jump out of the car and check our belongings. To my relief, everything was there and nothing seemed to be damaged.

We lugged everything into the airport and my eyes took in an amazing sight. Everything was perfectly calm. There were some people sitting in seats, but not many. I had heard that Baiyun Airport was one of the busiest airports in the country. How could that possibly be true?

We sat on the benches and waited for them to call our flight. Soon, more and more people came in. Then, they called our flight.

People seemed to pop out of nowhere. I felt like I was being attacked by a swarm of bees. They didn't need to heat the airport. The body heat going around was enough to burn through your skin. Now, I knew why it was one of the busiest airports.

When we had handed over our boarding passes and passed through the gate, instead of boarding the plane like we did in the U.S., we had to take a bus over to the plane. Then, we walked up the stairs and entered the plane.

Since this was new to me, I was very surprised when we got on the bus. When I saw the airplane, I couldn't believe it. Although I had ridden airplanes before, I had never touched the outside of a real, live plane.

When we finally arrived at Beijing Airport, the cold around me immediately chilled me to the bone. It was much, much colder than Guangzhou.

After retrieving our luggage, we headed for the exit. Just then, I heard a yell. I didn't even have to look to know to whom that voice belonged. It was Xu Laolao. I joyfully ran toward her and we exchanged joyful greetings. She introduced us to her son who was studying at Qinghua University, one of China's most prestigious universities.

Soon, a mini-van came driving up. The driver was Xu Laolao's friend. He was going to drive us to her house.

This airport was about thirty miles northeast of downtown Beijing so we had to drive close to an hour to get to Xu Laolao's apartment. Without fail, she started asking about her daughter who was a student at Texas University and a very close friend of ours. Xu Laolao had been to the U.S. about the same time as my grandmother had. That was why we knew her so well.

When we arrived at her apartment, Xu Laolao was very hospitable and asked us to have dinner with her. When I sat down at the table, the food swam before my eyes. I felt sick from the temperature change and the flight, so Xu Laolao hurriedly took me to bed. Within seconds, I was fast asleep...

December 8, 1992

We had a regular breakfast with dried preserves and rice. We also had tea. My parents were planning to go to a friend's house. Yan Yan lived in College Station and her parents lived in Beijing. We had brought a package with us from Yan Yan so we had to go to their house.

After breakfast, we piled on tons of sweaters and coats and set out. When I got out there, the cold came across me like thunder and my headache started again. I ignored it and listened to Xu Laolao.

Xu Laolao showed us the bus system and told us which bus to take. In Beijing, there were many different bus lines.

You could pay for your ticket every time or buy a bus ticket that lasted for a month. Since we weren't going to be in Beijing for that long, we bought tickets every time we got on the bus. The fare was fairly inexpensive so it didn't really matter. The price ranged from ten to thirty cents depending on the distance of the ride.

Suddenly, I felt the world flip upside down. The ground was in the place where the sky was supposed to be and the sky was where the ground was supposed to be.

I told my parents how I felt and they decided I needed to go home. Part of me wanted to go back but part of me wanted to go with them.

One part was saying, "Oh, my head."

The other part was saying, "My first day in Beijing and it's ruined."

In the end, my mom insisted that I go back.

Part of me was saying "Oh, I can't wait to get back in bed."

The other part was whining, "Mom..."

When we got back to the house, I took off my coat and scarf and sweater since I had a long-sleeved shirt and pants underneath. I felt too sick to even change. I just fell onto the sofa and was fast asleep before Xu Laolao had come back with a coverlet.

The next time I woke up, the television was on. Xu Laolao was on the phone and Ye-ye, her husband, was watching television. Since I couldn't fall asleep, I joined him.

Their television programs are just like the ones in the U.S. They have commercials, soap operas, music channels, movies, cartoons and talk shows.

Xu Laolao used to be a television director and the vice-director of Beijing Television Station. She is currently the General Secretary of the Chinese Association of TV Artists.

A television director and his secretary had just flown into Beijing that morning from Shenzhen, so Xu Laolao had invited them to dinner.

The director arrived with his very elegant secretary at six-thirty. Soon we were all seated. The dinner was delicious but the air around the table was a bit strained until the director started talking.

He had the most amazing things to tell us. He wasn't an heir to his money as I had imagined. In fact, he had been very poor. One day, he went to Shenzhen and bought a few shares of fairly inexpensive stock. That night, he stayed in a little motel. The next morning the price per share of the stock went up to the thousands, making him an instant millionaire.

After dinner, we had more tea around the table with Xu Laolao's best set of china. I kept thinking I was going to break the cup but fortunately I didn't. The cups were paper thin. If I had just rubbed my finger across it, it would probably shatter...

It is ten o'clock, and all the guests are finally leaving with a flurry of polite goodbyes. It is taking me tons of willpower not to collapse right on the sofa. My mom and I have unfolded it and made the bed. Tonight, I will sleep with my mom while Xu Laolao and Ye-ye sleep in their regular beds. My dad is already sleeping in Xu Laolao's son's bed.

December 9, 1992

Everyone is dressing warmly since we are planning to visit Mr. Xu Jianxin, the vice manager of the Continental Grand Hotel. He is one of Xu Laolao's business associates and friends.

As we stepped out into the morning freshness, we were welcomed by the sound of shoe soles. The children from the school across the street were having their morning run.

We took a taxi to the Continental Grand Hotel. When we arrived at the hotel, we climbed the spiralling staircase up to the second floor and found Mr. Xu's office.

We were anxious to see everything so we left his office and went downstairs. We went into a little bar where the adults had coffee and I had soda.

When I asked for a Sprite with ice, they were really surprised. They told me that the Sprite had just come out of the refrigerator.

After finishing our drinks, Mr. Xu gave us a tour of the hotel. When this hotel had been built, it was for the Asian Athletics Meet. At that time, all the competitors and their coaches stayed here. After the Meet, it had been remodeled a bit.

Soon, Mr. Xu led us into one of the fancier restaurants to have lunch which consisted mostly of duck. Beijing is famous for its roasted Peking duck.

After lunch, we talked for a short while in the lounge but my dad said that we really ought to be leaving since it was getting late. My dad exchanged business cards with Mr. Xu so they could keep in touch.

Tonight Xu Laolao and we were going to have dinner with the father of one of my dad's longtime friends, Mr. Li. When we were all ready to go, my mom gathered up the presents for Mr. Li, his wife, his daughter and his granddaughter. It was almost seven o'clock and we had agreed on meeting at six-thirty.

Upon arriving at their building, we went in the elevator to go to the fifth floor. There was a person working inside the elevator as an operator. When we got in, she didn't look too happy since we had invaded her quiet time.

When we finally got to their door, it was already seven-thirty. We were an hour late.

Mr. Li's family was very nice and they didn't complain about us being late. Mr. Li's wife went in the kitchen and started cooking while we were invited into the living room to talk.

The apartment was medium-sized, and it had one of everything – one bedroom, one living room, one dining room, one kitchen and one bathroom. The only thing that I thought was strange was that there were boxes piled to the ceiling in the dining room.

When we gave them the presents, they were really embarrassed and kept on thanking us. My parents quickly assured them that it had been no trouble on our part.

During dinner, they gave me a tiny bit of a very strong wine and I immediately felt the effects of it. They also encouraged me to drink a glass of beer. Although I refused, they kept on insisting. I finally told them that I didn't want to break the law. But after I had announced my fears, Mr. Li started laughing and laughing.

I didn't understand what was so funny. Finally, my dad told me that in China there were no restrictions on beer and wine. Although I still wasn't too comfortable, I forced myself to take one sip before giving the rest of it to my parents.

After dinner, my slightly dizzy brain and I went into the living room to rest. Xu Laolao and I made a phone call to her husband and son to tell them we would be getting home late.

Mr. Li never seemed to be short of things to talk about. I found out that he ran a company with Xu Laolao, Mr. Xu

Jianxin from the hotel and his daughter. The company is in Northeast China, dealing in a type of tea which would help lose weight. Mr. Li was manager, Xu Laolao and Mr. Xu were vice-managers.

The boxes I had seen in the dining room were filled with their tea. Mr. Li told us that the living room had also been filled but they had moved it to the balcony before our visit.

December 10, 1992

When I woke up, I found out my dad had gone to the Continental Grand Hotel, meeting with Mr. Xu. After breakfast, my mom and I were planning to go to Beihai Park. This park occupied the area that was once used as a garden by the Liao emperors. Kublai Khan chose this area as the site for his palace, which he built on the south bank of the lake. It was now known as the Round Town. Before leaving, though, my mom made me pile on sweaters, pants and coats.

When we got on the bus to Beihai Park, we had to pay ten cents. The bus wasn't very crowded so both my mom and I got a seat.

Later, during my stay in Beijing, I came to realize how lucky I had been that morning. Once we took a bus that was so crowded the conductor had to force the people in and slam the door shut. I ended up having footprints on my back because people had actually put their feet on my back when I bent down.

The reason I continued taking buses in Beijing after that was that I think taking buses is part of everyday life. I wanted to know exactly what it would feel like living in Beijing. Anyway, I think riding the bus is a very interesting and exciting experience.

We got off at a stop and transferred to another bus which would take us directly to the front gates of Beihai Park. The transfer was quick and easy. Soon, we were standing outside the park.

One of the first things I saw was a big lake with a bridge over it. At the end of the bridge, I saw a pagoda. Hidden behind it in the trees was Bai Ta or The White Dagoba.

I saw buddhas all around the park but my favorite one was the white jade Buddha in Chengguang Dian, Hall of Inherited Lustre. The pagodas and towers were painted in vivid colors, but they had badly faded.

My mom and I followed a path by the stream to a lake. The temperature was close to zero so the lake was half frozen. I was chilled to the bone despite all the clothes I had on. I followed my mom down the path and pretty soon, the Bai Ta came into sight. I had heard so much about this place that my head swiveled as I tried to take in everything at once.

Two small towers stood in front of the Dagoba with worn steps leading up to them. I slowly climbed up and looked around. Both towers had beautifully painted ceilings with red, blue, green and yellow designs.

When we came out of the tower, we found ourselves very close to the Dagoba. There was a stone tablet in front of us. It told me tons of information about the Dagoba so I got out a piece of paper and recorded everything.

Erected in 1651, the dagoba stands 35.9 meters high. The dagoba was twice badly shaken by earthquakes which occurred respectively in 1679 and 1730 and was rebuilt on both occasions. In the subsequent years, the dagoba had been given regular maintenance. It was reinforced and overhauled in 1974. The upper part of the dagoba, "the thirteen heavens" collapsed during the 1976 Tangshan earthquake and was rebuilt in the next year.

After a brief lunch, we were off in search of Tiantan, or the Temple of Heaven. We had the bad luck to ask a bicycle rickshaw driver where it was.

I think he suspected we weren't from Beijing, because he told us a whole bunch of nonsense. He offered to take us to the front entrance for only eight dollars. Since he had made it sound so complicated, we thought it was a good deal so we immediately agreed to it.

I had always wanted to ride on a bicycle rickshaw anyway. We soon realized our mistake. We could have taken a bus which would have taken us directly to the front entrance of the park, and it would have just cost us twenty cents. He had pedalled us around in circles to make the ride seem longer. So much for the excitement of rickshaw riding.

The Temple of Heaven was built in 1426. It was where the emperors of the Ming and Qing dynasties worshipped the heavens. Beijing is a city of many temples. The one that stands out from the rest of them in its perfection is the Temple of Heaven.

Its reputation as the most beautiful single piece of creation in all of China is a well-deserved one. The Temple of Heaven is said to be most impressive by moonlight but I didn't get to see it at night.

My favorite place in the temple was Echo Wall. Anything I said would come back again. Even my slightest whispers.

After our visit there, we ate dinner in one of the little restaurants along the street. We had noodle soup which was very spicy. When we finished dinner, my mom and I walked out to find the bus stop. The first bus that came was so crowded that we couldn't get on. We had to wait another five minutes for the next bus to come.

I was glad to have spent the whole day with my mom, exploring China's capital. It wasn't a surprise that we were tired out by the time we got home.

December 11, 1992

Mr. Gao, Xu Laolao's company chaffeur, had promised to
take us to Yuanming Yuan this morning. He arrived a few
minutes after we got dressed. My mom and I got in the car
and soon, we were off.

Yuanming Yuan, the Garden of Perfect Brightness, is also
known as the Old Summer Palace. After its destruction by
British and French troops in 1860, it was never rebuilt. The
ruins were the only thing that could be seen today.

It was a long drive since Yuanming Yuan was in the north-
west suburbs. When we got there, Mr. Gao offered to wait
for us and take us home afterwards. We quickly assured him
that it wasn't necessary. We didn't want to waste his time.

We paid the fee to get in and then entered the park. We
wanted to see the place called Yizhi, or ruins, which the British and French had set ablaze. At first, we walked around at
a leisurely pace. The scenery was beautiful and we took many
pictures.

I wanted to find Yizhi soon and see if it was as spectacular as everyone had said. My mom and I searched and
searched but we couldn't find it.

We walked onto another path and soon came into a little
clearing. Two people sitting in lawn chairs were talking in
Chinese. They were selling tickets to go on a dragon tram to
Yizhi. We paid for round-trip tickets and sat down and waited
for the tram. In less than two minutes it arrived. The front of
the tram was a dragon head and the back was a tail. Everybody piled in and we were on our way.

After dodging past some trees, we finally came in view
of the Yizhi. It was breathtakingly picturesque. Now I knew
what everybody had been oohing and aahing over when the
topic of the Yizhi was brought up.

I was aching to get some pictures of it. I wish I could

have brought it to America for all my friends to see. It was so different from anything else I had seen in my life.

We went in and walked on the actual stone structure. It was really high so my mom didn't go to the very top with me. After I had seen enough, my mom and I got back on the tram.

It wasn't until after I came home that I realized Yuanming Yuan was my favorite park. It seemed so pure. The fact that the Empress Dowager didn't spend any money to repair it made it seem even more beautiful. It transported me from the modern world to the old world where the emperors and empresses ruled the land.

We left Yuanming Yuan at lunch time.

After a simple meal, we got on the bus to the Beijing Zoo, one of the most widely-visited sites in Beijing along with the Forbidden City. Most people go there to see the pandas. I wanted to see every animal there was.

When I got off the bus, I realized how little I knew about zoos and animals. I had not been to a zoo for so long, I could hardly remember what it would be like. The town we lived in didn't have a zoo so I rarely had a chance to visit one.

My mom bought the tickets and we entered the zoo with a map in our hands. First, we visited the different birds, then the monkeys. The monkeys were living on a little hill that was surrounded by tall walls.

When I got to the wall, I was scared out of my wits. A monkey had somehow climbed up to the railing. Then he reached the top of the wall. We were both surprised. The monkey and I stared at each other without moving for a few seconds. When I finally came out of my reverie and shook my head, the monkey started moving. My mom and I watched the monkey play for a while, before he fell back down the wall.

Next we went to see the tigers and lions. They looked vicious with their sharp jaws.

Then we went to see the bears. I think the polar bear was the cutest. We saw all the animals in the next few hours. My favorite was the seal. It kept on doing little tricks for us in the water. I didn't really like the elephants because their stalls smelled horrible. The pandas were cute, too.

By the time we were done looking at the animals, it was time to go. However, my mom and I had to use the restroom first. When we went in the restroom, there were a few people sitting around smoking.

"Sorry, the bathroom gets off work in one minute," one of the men explained.

I choked back my laughter.

"The bathroom gets off work?" my mom repeated.

"Yeah, its business hours are from nine to five," he answered.

My mom and I ran out of there as fast as we could. The minute we were outside, we burst out laughing. That a bathroom ever got off work was funny enough, but the fact that it had business hours was just too much.

When we were through laughing, we left to find another restroom with better hours.

December 12, 1992

The cold air is starting to get to me. It seems that Beijing's wind and cold never go away. I do not know how people survive in Beijing with this freezing temperature every single day. As usual, I am wrapped tightly in clothes but the cold seems to be able to seep through even the thickest of material. Today we're going to the Summer Palace.

I couldn't wait. Cold or not, I had always wanted to go to Yihe Yuan, the Summer Palace. My dad was also coming with us since he thought that Yihe Yuan was one of the more special places in Beijing. He wanted to take pictures.

In 1880, the British and French destroyed Yihe Yuan but the Empress Dowager rebuilt it in 1888, allegedly with money that should have gone to building up the Chinese Navy. The Empress Dowager was the last real ruler of the Qing dynasty and has been known for her cruelty.

Yihe Yuan is a fairly big park that covers over five hundred ninety hectares. Unfortunately, the only standing pavilions left are the Bronze Pavilion and the Sea of Wisdom Temple. On major holidays, the park is decorated as it would have been for Empress Dowager's birthday with lanterns, flags, special displays of potted plants.

We took a mini-bus to Yihe Yuan. I settled back and tried to enjoy the scenery around me. Beijing may be notable for its cold weather, but it is a city that should certainly also be known for its beautiful scenery. I would happily welcome some of Beijing's characteristics in America, but I wouldn't be able to live in this freezing city.

I got off the bus first. I do not know why none of the parks we had visited so far had a fancy exterior. It is almost as if the emperors and empresses spent so much money on the interior, they forgot there was an exterior.

My mom went over to buy the tickets for us while my dad and I looked at the map and introduction to the park. I learned a lot of things. The park was one of the Empress Dowager's favorites and she often visited it. When the park was destroyed a second time in 1900, she had it rebuilt in 1902, demanding progress reports every five days. The park has not been changed much since the rebuilding in 1902 but the timberwork has been constantly repainted.

We entered the park and saw a huge ice-filled lake in front of us. Behind it, there was a never-ending supply of trees. A huge pagoda stood out of it. It was beautiful. I continued to stare at it without knowing what to say. It had never occurred to me that this park would be so beautiful. It seemed to fit its name perfectly. I could just imagine what it would look like in the summer.

We went through the park slowly, stopping at every pagoda and temple. It was extremely crowded, even on the lake. People were skating and strolling on the ice.

I enjoyed wandering through the park and looking at the different pagodas and temples. There were two things that really aroused my interest. One was the Chang Lang, or the Long Corridor.

Chang Lang is an extremely long corridor. On the ceilings of this corridor are brightly painted pictures. Every set of pictures tells a Chinese story. Two of the stories I have already read are Dream of the Red Mansions and Outlaws of the Marsh.

The other point of interest was a little temple-like building where Empress Dowager Cixi had imprisoned her son, Emperor Guangxu.

The Empress Dowager had locked the emperor in a room with no windows. The walls were as hard as granite. It was almost like a prison. The emperor led a reform movement,

*which threatened the Empress Dowager's authority. How-
ever, the reform movement failed. The Empress Dowager
imprisoned the emperor and assumed supreme power herself.*

After wandering through the park for a while, we went
out one of the side exits to have lunch.

We found a slightly run-down restaurant and decided to
go in. The waitress/owner was at the door welcoming us in.

There were a few tables inside the small room, where a
man was eating noodles while reading the newspaper. My
dad looked at the menu posted on the wall and then ordered.
The food didn't turn out to be that great but the hospitality
made up for it.

The owner told us a little about herself. She was only
twenty seven years old and had opened this little restaurant
about a year ago. What set us laughing was that her husband
was a soldier. In China, Communists and Capitalists were
against each other. A soldier was supposed to fight for the
Communist cause and any kind of entrepreneur would be
considered a Capitalist. Imagine the marriage of a Communist to a Capitalist.

Then she asked about us. She said we didn't look like
Beijing residents. I guess my dad thought it would do no
harm to tell her who we were. The moment we said the magic
word, "America," the man at the other table put down his
newspaper and came over to introduce himself.

He was the vice-manager of a company and wanted to
know if we wanted to do some business with him. I kind of
doubted it because he wasn't really dressed properly. If he
was the vice-manager of a company, why in the world would
he be eating in a restaurant like this? When he showed us his
business card, I realized my mistake. I had always hated
people who judged people by their appearances only. I was
very ashamed because that was exactly what I had done.

My dad talked to the man for a while but he wasn't really
interested in doing business.

When we finished our meal, we left the restaurant and we got on another mini-bus to Tiananmen. We were planning to see the Forbidden City this afternoon.

On the mini-bus, I was so tired I fell asleep. When I woke up, we were nearing Tiananmen. We stopped at the red light. In the middle of the street were traffic lights. A policeman was standing under them.

The car next to us raced past the red light so the policeman ran up and tried to stop the driver. But instead of pulling over, the driver accelerated the car while rolling down the window vigorously and thrust three oranges at the policeman.

"Want some oranges?" he yelled.

The policeman was kind of surprised so he waved the driver. I couldn't believe how fast that man had been driving. I was still puzzling over why the driver threw oranges at the policeman when we were let off on the corner of the street.

Tiananmen looks exactly like it does in pictures. I cannot say I am overly impressed. The huge portrait of Chairman Mao at the front of the main gate is very majestic-looking.

The interior is very different from what I had previously imagined it to be. Storefronts are lined on the sides of the walls. People are streaming in and out of the stores. It is more like a zoo than the peaceful haven I had imagined it would be.

My dad suggested we go to the top of Tiananmen. My mom didn't come with us because she wanted to look around in the stores.

My dad and I climbed up the stairs to the terrace. While he was taking pictures, I tried to imagine what it would feel like if I were Chairman Mao up there.

I remembered a story my dad had once told me. It was about his uncle.

"In China, the Communists took over in 1949. Practically everything was under their control. They divided people into good and bad. There were five classes of good people and five classes of bad people. The bad people were classed as landlords, wealthy farmers, anti-Revolutionists, very bad people and Rightists.

My uncle's immediate family was pretty 'bad.' My uncle owned only a small piece of land, but he was still considered a landlord. They also said he was a Rightist. His older brother was arrested and accused of being an anti-Revolutionist because he used to be a colonel in the Kuomintang Army.

People were taught to be loyal to Chairman Mao. Kids in school were taught to do whatever he instructed. Those who dared to speak out against him were usually killed or arrested. Many decided at a young age to become Red Guards and protect Chairman Mao. They believed that their duty as citizens was to protect Mao from any harm.

It wasn't much of a surprise that my cousin wanted to be a Red Guard. Since he was from a 'bad' family, he thought he was very lucky to have the opportunity to be a Red Guard. The minute he received the news he raced to Beijing to see Chairman Mao.

Meanwhile, in his hometown, his father, my uncle, was still a lecturer at a technical school. Since he was from a 'bad' family, the students didn't respect him. They got away with everything. They hit him, they tripped him, they spat at his feet and sometimes, they even spat in his face.

Many of these students were Red Guards so they came to his house one night when his son was in Beijing. They ransacked the house and looked through everything. They were looking for anything that would show how bad he was.

Since his brother used to be a colonel in the Kuomintang Army, his mother had kept the Kuomintang army uniform. When the Red Guards saw this, they were extremely pleased. This was good, hard evidence that he was a traitor.

They made my uncle put on the uniform. He also had to wear a wooden box around his neck. Anti-Revolutionist was *printed in huge, bold letters on the box. They took him and made him walk down the streets to the school where he taught. The Red Guards beat him until he was covered with blood. Then, they threw him in jail.*

At the time of his beating and arrest, his son was standing in the middle of Tiananmen Square yelling, 'Long live Chairman Mao!'"

That was not all. My father's uncle, or Gu Ye had yet another sad story in his painful life.

"In the late 1960's, Gu Ye was taken to the countryside for brainwashing," said my father. "He was made to endure the most terrible work conditions. However, he soon earned his place among the county members.

"He had been a teacher at a technical college and he knew a lot about engineering so he designed several small electrical generators for his county and surrounding counties. China's countryside was extremely primitive back then so they didn't have many sources of electricity. This generator supplied electricity for the entire county. Soon, they were being sold throughout the country and even exported to some foreign countries.

"Gu Ye and his invention soon became famous throughout the area. One night, the county held a science conference and the mayor spoke out about him. He scattered praise all over the modest man while the audience listened with awe and respect. Gu Ye was the next to take the platform.

"It had to have been the excitement. All his life, he had been pushed away because he was 'bad.' Now, he was being praised by a very influential man, applauded by a spellbound audience and given the chance to speak in front of a large crowd of people.

"He paused in front of the podium. He stared out at the crowd with bright eyes. Five seconds later, he was falling to the ground. It was his first stroke.

"A woman sitting on the stage quickly supported him and

held him up. Her father had died from a stroke so she knew
that Gu Ye wasn't supposed to lie down. If it had not been for
her, Gu Ye would have had thirteen years cut off from his life.

"After recovering from his stroke, his right side was para-
lyzed. He had to learn to use a wheelchair, write with his left
hand and adjust to a whole different way of life. However,
for a man as strong as him, this didn't matter. He adjusted to
his partial paralysis and soon he was doing the same things
as before.

"It is people like him that we should truly admire. He was
born into a 'bad' family but that didn't stop him. He was
discriminated against because of his background but he ac-
complished more than most people from 'good' families.
Later, when he was partially paralyzed, he still continued
on. Do you think you could have done the same, my daugh-
ter?"

I went into a room on the balcony. They were selling souvenirs there. I got two necklaces. One had Tiananmen on
one side and a rooster on the other. The second necklace had
Tiananmen and a pig which I was planning to give to my
cousin. She was born in the year of the pig and I was born in
the year of the rooster.

After coming down, my mom informed me that she had
seen some signs saying that there was a wax museum. I had
never seen a wax museum, so we decided to visit it.

Inside, the lights were dim but I could still see the wax
figures. They looked incredibly real. There were wax figures
of famous men and women including Confucius and Emperor Qin Shi Huang, the first emperor in Chinese history.

When we came out, it was already four thirty so we hurriedly went over to the entrance of the Forbidden City. For
some reason, there was a barricade at the entrance. My dad
asked the woman standing near the exit. She told us that the
Forbidden City was closed already. I couldn't believe it! We
would have to visit it another time.

We headed toward the gate. To our surprise, everybody had stopped in front of the gate. There was a lot of pushing and cursing going on. I couldn't see what had happened, so I tried to push my way up to the front.

The soldiers were lowering the Chinese flag.

Every day, at eight o'clock in the morning, the soldiers would march out to Tiananmen Square to raise the flag. At five in the afternoon, they would lower it. The soldiers were making their way back now. People got out of the way while they jogged back. One soldier was in charge of the flag and he held it up high above his head while they jogged.

We took a bus back to Xu Laolao's apartment. It was so crowded that my mom didn't even have enough room to reach in her pocket to get the money to buy tickets.

I gritted my teeth and stood there without moving, even when people pushed me. Finally, my dad yelled for me to get off at the next stop. When the bus stopped again, I jumped off.

The first thing my dad said when he shoved his way off the bus was that he would never ride on a bus again. He usually didn't take buses so he had no idea what my mom and I had gone through every day since our arrival.

When we got back, Xu Laolao was impatiently waiting for us. She reminded us of the theater tickets she had gotten. We had completely forgotten about them, and Mr. Gao was picking us up anytime now. In actuality, I wasn't interested in watching a Chinese play but my dad insisted that I watch one. I wasn't so sure. I thought I would be bored to death since I wouldn't be able to understand most of it.

We drove through many streets. Most of them were vacant and spooky. It had started raining in the middle of our drive to the theater. The rain seemed to make everything so much drearier.

After quite a while, a huge three-story building came into sight. It didn't look like a theater to me but we had swerved into the parking lot in front of it.

Our family and Xu Laolao entered the building while Mr. Gao left to park the car. I looked around curiously. This wasn't the way a theater was supposed to look.

When we entered, two marble columns and a huge carpeted staircase welcomed us. We went in the snack shop to get something to eat during the play. My mom got some juice and cookies. It didn't take me long to find out that Chinese people do not eat popcorn.

Xu Laolao led us up the stairway into the theater. The lights were dim. Mr. Gao found our seats. They were pretty much on the side so we couldn't see the stage too well. My dad handed me a program.

The name of the play was *Xiao Jing Hu Tong*, or Little Street with a Well. What kind of title was that? Were they going to tell us the life story of a well?

Soon, the lights started dimming, one by one. I expected to hear some kind of announcer telling us the title of the play and some background information but to my surprise, the curtains just opened and a scene started.

At first, all I could figure out was what was before my eyes. I saw a little girl, an old man, a tree and a well. As the play went on, I finally caught on to it. It was about the lives of the families that lived on a street before, during and after the Cultural Revolution.

Although I figured out what it was about, I still had no earthly idea what they were talking about. Most of the words they used were too complicated for me. In about ten sentences, I could make out a few pronouns and nouns. My dad also told me that one of the reasons I couldn't understand was that they used a lot of jargon that was common during the Cultural Revolution. My parents and everybody else were able to understand because they had experienced the Cultural Revolution.

The only way I knew how I was supposed to react was by listening to other people's reactions. Whenever they laughed, I knew that whatever line the person had said was funny.

Whenever they looked grim, it was either a sad or just a regular line. How in the world was I supposed to understand a play based on that? Pretty soon, my head was on my mom's shoulder and I was fast asleep.

December 13, 1992

The Great Wall of China is said to be the only manmade
structure that could be seen from the moon with the naked
eye. Accounts in some books contradict that statement. After
I saw the Great Wall, I was more than willing to believe it.

Work on the wall began when the State of Chu needed a
fortification. Many other states copied the wall. Some of these
walls are now said to be a few thousand li long.

The first emperor of Qin extended it to ten thousand li
long. This is where the name Wanli Changcheng came from.
Wanli Changcheng means ten thousand li long wall so they
began calling it the Great Wall of China.

During the Han dynasty, it was extended to the Gobi
Desert because people needed to protect their far-reaching
land but the Han and the Qin weren't the only dynasties that
helped build the Great Wall. The wall was strengthened and
further extended during the Jing and Ming dynasties. In fact,
much of what can be seen today are the improvements made
during the Ming dynasty. The Great Wall now consists of
bricks but before the Ming dynasty, it was made of tamped
earth.

I couldn't wait to see the Great Wall for myself. I wanted
to see if the pictures and stories of it did the wall justice.
Another part of me felt a twinge of guilt as I thought about
all the people who died building it.

I still remember a story from one of my kindergarten
classes in China:

Once upon a time, there were two old married couples.
They were neighbors and they were nice people. The only
thing that made their lives incomplete was that neither couple
had any children.

One day, one of the men got some pumpkin seeds and

planted one on each side of the fence which separated the two couples. Strangely, pumpkins wouldn't grow. Vines grew out of the place where the seed had been but not a single pumpkin. The vines finally grew to the top of the fence. Then, they intertwined and a few days later, a pumpkin started growing. It got bigger and bigger and it wouldn't stop growing.

The two couples were very alarmed. They thought it was the devil trying to scare them. They tried to think of ways to stop it from growing, but there seemed to be no other way than chopping it up. They got together one evening and cut down the pumpkin. They chopped it open. When they looked inside, to their surprise, they saw a little baby girl staring at them.

She was a beautiful baby and the two couples were delighted. They finally had a child to look after. They shared the baby and the baby girl grew bigger and bigger.

Many years later, the girl was a young lady ready to be married. Her parents found a wonderful husband for her. They got married and they lived very happily together but one day her husband was called upon to help build the Great Wall. She was very upset but she knew they had no choice. They exchanged many good-byes and her husband left.

Three years drifted slowly by. She grew more and more depressed. One day, she decided to go look for her husband. She lived very far away from the Great Wall, and she had to make the journey on foot.

After walking for almost two weeks, she reached the wall. She inquired about her husband but nobody knew anything. She walked almost the whole distance of the wall, asking after her husband. On the fifth day, a man who knew her husband told her he had died from a disease.

She could swallow her grief no longer. She cried and cried. It is said that the gods heard her. At that moment, the Great Wall sank into the ground. She jumped in to join her husband.

After she jumped in, the Great Wall grew up again. It became as strong as their love for each other had been and still is.

This is one of my favorite stories.

We had breakfast and dressed quickly. Mr. Gao was going to take us to Badaling – the most famous tourist spot on the Great Wall, which was a little more than fifty kilometers north of central Beijing. We had a long drive ahead, therefore I decided to take a nap during the drive.

When I opened my eyes, I was surprised to see the mountains and the narrow roads in front of us. These roads were dangerous. If we had just driven a little bit off mark, we could have wound up at the bottom of a gorge. This was one time when I definitely would have preferred to be walking.

We finally got to the gates of the Great Wall. Everyone breathed a sigh of relief and I caught my first glimpse of the Great Wall. It was spectacular – everything that had been said about it had not come close to the reality.

After purchasing some fur capes from a nearby souvenir shop, we started climbing the Great Wall. As we got higher, we were slowly enveloped by the cold. We were at a very high elevation now. The temperature was below zero. It didn't take long for Mr. Gao and my dad to figure out that the fur capes were made out of fake fur.

I climbed and climbed, stopping occasionally to admire the scenery. It was truly beautiful. Suddenly, the mountains didn't seem like my enemies anymore. In fact, they were more like friends. Everything seemed so pure up there. It was true mountain air.

Pretty soon, the steps became farther apart so I had to strain to climb them. My energy was slowly being sapped. I really wanted to get to the very top but when I told my parents of my goal, they said it was impossible. In fact, we were pretty high up already. There weren't many people around at this height.

My dad soon told us we were going to start on our way down. I tried to protest but he wouldn't give in. He reminded me how scared I had been at first. Up there, we would be all by ourselves.

Finally, I convinced him to let me climb up to the next pavilion. When we got up there, there were vendors selling souvenirs and certificates certifying that you had climbed the Great Wall. Since most of the people didn't get up here, not a lot of people got this certificate. I decided to buy one for myself. While we were up there somebody told us that this was where the president of the United States had stopped, too.

It was really starting to get cold at that point. I didn't have my mittens so my fingers were half frozen. My face looked like a tomato. It was so red from the cold.

We started down in high spirits but I was soon apprehensive again. The steps were really far apart. Once, I almost fell down the steps because of the ice on the ground. It was much harder going down than going up. I was glad my dad had not let me go up to the very top but I wasn't about to admit it to him.

There were some steps coming up to the side of the wall so I got curious and climbed down. To my delight, there was a camel and a horse there that we could get on and take pictures with. I got on the camel, and before I had even gotten comfortable, he started clicking away.

When we finally climbed down all the stairs, I looked back up at the Great Wall. On the wall, I had not thought we had gone a long way but when I looked up at it again, I realized how far and high we had walked.

I bought a few souvenirs from one of the storefronts. Meanwhile, my dad was urging me to hurry because we were going to the Ming Tombs or Shisan Ling (Thirteen Tombs) next. The Ming Tombs are rather close to the Great Wall, so we decided to visit both in the same day.

The Ming Tombs are where the Ming emperors are buried. Each one of them has a tomb to himself. There were sixteen Ming emperors, but only thirteen were buried here.

Among the thirteen tombs, Chang Ling (Long-lasting Tomb) and Ding Ling (Stable Tomb) are the only two open to public.

We only got to see Ding Ling. Since it was underground, we had to go down many flights of stairs. When we reached the bottom, the first thing we saw was a huge stone door. The door was open but it made me feel really uncomfortable.

It is said that when the emperor ordered this tomb to be made, he had workers hide arrows behind the walls. If anybody tried to get in and succeeded, the deadly arrows would come shooting out at him. I wondered what happened to the first person who had opened the door. Had he been shot with the arrows? Did he die?

There was a huge corridor beyond the doors. At the end of it were some corridors and we went down one of them. We entered a room that held three huge coffins. They were brown and ugly. I immediately realized they were just copies. The one in the middle was bigger than the other ones. Since an emperor and two empresses were buried here, I guessed the one in the middle must be the emperor's coffin and the smaller ones were the empresses.

We went through the entire tomb. I think it is terrible that they buried real, live people with him so he could have servants in heaven. They also buried jewels, gold and silver with the emperors so they would have enough to spend in their afterlife.

December 14, 1992

It was unlike any other morning. I actually didn't want to leave the apartment! Unfortunately, my mom and I had to go to the train station to buy tickets to Shanghai.

When we set out, the temperature was still below zero. The air was crisp and cold. We got on a bus that took us to the train station.

The train station was built in the 1950's, and it is the only one in Beijing, so I was pretty sure it would be like Guangzhou's. I imagined it would be horribly crowded and disgusting. I was partly right.

Outside, it was crowded and noisy but inside it was completely different from Guangzhou's train station. It was much bigger. Only the odor was a problem. When we entered the station, I noticed a foul odor. At first I thought it was someone who had forgotten to put on their deodorant, but I soon realized it was a permanent stench.

My mom went up to the booth to buy tickets, and before I could think about anything else, she came back with three tickets for the day after next.

We left the train station in a hurry because we couldn't wait to get back into the fresh air. The bus took us to Tiananmen, where we were planning on seeing the Forbidden City again. This time, we went straight past the gates of Tiananmen without dawdling. We passed through Wumen which is considered the front gate to the Forbidden City.

Whenever the emperor decided to kill somebody, he would command his guards to push the person out of Wumen. The minute the person was out, one of the guards would swing the sword and cut off the person's head. The reason they didn't do this inside was that they thought it would pollute the Forbidden City.

The first thing we saw when we entered the Forbidden City were five marble bridges. There wasn't a lake or body of water in sight. It was just for decoration! Before us stood Taihe Dian, or The Hall of Supreme Harmony. Leading up to the hall was a large carved ramp. On either side of the ramp were two sets of stairs.

I could just imagine the emperor being carried in his sedan chair over the ramp while the carriers walked on the stairs beside him. The ramp had carved pictures of a dragon which represented the emperor. If anybody accidentally stepped on the ramp, it would be out of Wumen and off with his head. Now, with no emperor around to cut off their heads, little children were running over it with wild enthusiasm.

We continued touring through the Forbidden City. Everything was so peaceful – just as the old days must have been. I tried to imagine myself being both the emperor and one of his servants.

While we walked through the city, we would occasionally stop and look at the private apartments which were open to tourists. The Forbidden City had pagodas, temples, halls and pavilions but I didn't take pleasure and interest in going' through these like I had at Yuanming Yuan, Beihai and the other parks – even when we visited the Imperial Garden. The trees there were said to be the original ones but I kind of doubted it.

We started our walk back. To me, the whole Forbidden City seemed so fake. So many people had died here because of the selfishness of the many generations of emperors and empresses.

It was after we had exited the city that I began to be cheerful again. The only impression the Forbidden City had left with me was a bad one. It also seemed that darkness and age were clouding over my perceptions.

My mom set a brisk pace since we were going to Wangfujing Street, one of the busiest streets in Beijing. We were going to visit one of the bookstores there so I could buy some books.

There was a McDonald's on the corner of Wangfujing. I was pretty surprised to see one here. It looked like any McDonald's in America. We walked down the street looking at the shops. There were a wide variety of stores including supermarkets, bookstores, miscellaneous stores, computer companies and music stores. There were also a huge crowd of people along the streets. I bet a lot of tourists came to this street just to see the crowd.

We went in the first bookstore but there were no books in English. After finding out where the foreign language book-store was, we decided to go to have a look. Carts were roll-ing past. People were shoving us aside. I finally realized we weren't going to get out of the crowd if we didn't push a little ourselves. My mom and I seemed to get the same idea at the same time. We started shoving like crazy. Nobody said anything. I guess they were used to it.

After doing some book shopping we got on the bus. We had to hurry home since Xu Laolao had especially asked us to come home early for dinner. I think she was kind of mad that we weren't having many meals at her house. She had informed us in the morning that we were having *huoguo* (Mongolian hot pot) tonight, and that she wanted us to be on time.

Xu Laolao was still in the kitchen preparing for dinner when we arrived. My dad still wasn't home yet. I was so hungry I wanted to grab the pot and start eating. I wanted to kill my dad when he got back. Had he forgotten about our plans?

At that moment someone knocked on the door. It was my dad. He came in the kitchen and began helping Xu Laolao cut the meat and peel the shrimp.

Finally, we were called to the dinner table, and all six of us were present. During the meal, everybody was too involved in eating to talk much.

After our very filling dinner, we went into the living room and talked. My mom and I then told them about the train tickets. Xu Laolao said she was glad that we were able to get the tickets but she wished we would stay for a few more days.

December 15, 1992

After spending the first part of our morning trying to sell our laptop, I got to spend some time with my dad. We were hungry and it was about lunch time so we decided to eat at one of the streetside cafes that were everywhere. We sat down at the table and ordered some noodles.

The noodles we ordered were of a special type. The way it was made was extremely weird. First, they took a long piece of dough. Then, they would stretch it and swing it, stretch and swing. Finally, they would have a very long and thin piece of dough. Then, they would cut it into many pieces and boil it. This was a way of making noodles called *la mian*. *La* means stretched and *mian* means noodles.

Since Beijingers like to eat it hot and spicy, they had a jar of sauce for us. Just a tiny portion of the sauce would make your eyes water and your tongue burn.

I learned about these hot sauces the hard way. I had a whole spoonful of the sauce on my spoon. My dad caught me just as I was about to dump the whole spoonful into my noodles. He made me put in a tiny little bit of what I had originally intended, which was enough to make my mouth scream for water.

After lunch, we went to the Board of Education where Zhang Ling, my dad's friend, worked. He had asked us to meet him there. We were going to see a performance by an art ensemble which was bound for the U.S.

When we arrived at his office, Mr. Zhang was on the phone. He gestured toward us and yelled, "My friends!"

After coming out of the building, Mr. Zhang told us about the ensemble that was going to the United States. It consisted of performers who sang, danced and acted out plays. They would be visiting many U.S. cities. Today they were performing here.

As we softly entered the auditorium, they were in the

middle of a play. This type of play is called *Xiaopin* (mini comedy). It was an extremely funny story about a man and his daughter-in-law. The man was Chinese and his daughter-in-law was American. The actress was Chinese, but she was wearing a blonde wig. The two fought incessantly about different things because of their different cultures, and to make matters worse, they didn't understand each other at all.

Toward the end, the girl gave her father-in-law a robe.

"What's this?" he asked.

"It's a present for you. It's called a robe. You sleep in it at night," she answered.

"What? You have to wear clothes when you sleep?" he asked incredulously.

Everybody burst into laughter at this statement and the actor and actress took their bows. As they left the stage, the curtain came thundering down.

The next act was a dance, and it was beautiful. In the middle of this dance, Mr. Zhang went up to the second row and began talking with someone. Then, he came back up and told us we could go sit up in the second row. The person he had been speaking with turned out to be his wife. My dad and I sat down next to her but Mr. Zhang told us he had to leave.

When his wife saw me, she gave me some Chinese snacks to eat. The view from the second row was much better than where we had been sitting.

Then there was a singer. Her song was very pretty but her shrill voice hurt my eardrums. That was the last act, so when it finished, we left the auditorium. Mr. Zhang's wife offered us a ride home.

After dinner, my dad said that he felt like going to see the opera. We were leaving the next day and we still had not seen real Peking opera.

We left the apartment and flagged down a bicycle rickshaw. The driver recommended Qianmen Hotel for quality opera. In fact, he said it was the only place where we would be able to see Peking opera that night, so my dad told the driver to step on it.

The driver was very amusing. He told us that he used to be the special driver for an opera singer who sang at the Qianmen Hotel and that all he had to do was to take the man to and from work. He was free to do anything he wished for the rest of the day. What a life! The opera star had lived to the the ripe old age of eighty-seven, and he had died singing.

When we got to the theater, there was nobody there to sell tickets so we went straight in. Inside, there was a balcony-turned stage. Below the stage were tables and chairs which made the whole place look like a nightclub. Only a few foreigners sat at these tables, sipping tea and watching the performance. I was extremely disappointed. Did Chinese people not enjoy Peking opera?

I loved it! Peking Opera is a true feast for the senses. The performers were dressed in bright, colorful costumes and their faces were painted like masks. They sang and danced, and - I had never in my life seen anything like this - the performers kept on doing flips and jumps. It was so unlike any other kind of opera I had seen on TV. I could have watched it forever. Unfortunately, the show ended in less than twenty minutes.

I was starting to believe that Chinese people didn't like Chinese culture. I think Peking opera is a very interesting part of Chinese history. Yet, the Chinese people seemed so caught up in things like new movie releases.

China seemed to be improving in its attempts to modernize, but its culture seemed to be slowly disappearing. China has one of the most interesting histories in the world. If it was neglected, it would slowly be forgotten.

My dad told me that in earlier years, Peking opera was available every night and everywhere in Beijing. What happened to it? Why did we only find one place? Where were all the people who used to enjoy it?

A year earlier, The Chinese Song and Dance Troupe came

to College Station, Texas. The performance was a great hit and everybody was impressed. However, a few weeks after they had left, the China Club newsletter printed an article assaulting almost every single performer in the troupe. The author wrote that Peking opera was a "deformed art," and that it should not even be called an art. I wanted to tell him that he had a deformed mind and that he should not be called a person.

In bookstores, I had wanted to find some books that would tell me more about Chinese culture. My dad had also tried to find books like that in Chinese. He had even less luck than me. He told me that all he saw were bestsellers, thrillers, romances and murder mysteries.

Was China slowly starting to go downhill? Did people no longer remember the history of the country they lived in? Did they no longer enjoy older traditions? Some people think old means bad. That is nonsense. I enjoy bestsellers, but I love to read books that teach me culture, too. I enjoy movies but I also love Peking opera. It is definitely not a deformed art.

When we came out of the theater, we saw a little shop that smelled of incense. My dad and I went in.

I bought a souvenir that was on extremely thin paper. If I had rubbed my fingers across it a few times, it would have torn. On it was a painting of a performer in full costume and makeup. To this day, I still do not know how they managed to paint on the paper in such fine detail.

My dad picked out a souvenir, too. It was a small Chinese instrument called the *jinghu* (two stringed fiddle). It is used regularly for opera music. My dad knew how to play it and he wanted one so he could practice in America.

The salesman observed us for a while. Then he started getting curious and asked us several questions but my dad didn't answer the questions until they finished bargaining for the instrument.

My dad planned on telling them where we were from, but if they had known we were from the United States, they would have thought we had tons of money, and they would have charged us twice the real price.

After he had paid, he answered the man's inquiry by telling him we were from the United States. When he got to where we were from, everybody seemed to freeze at the word, the "United States." In less than ten seconds, one of the salesclerks was trying to tell me how great every product in the store was.

I ignored her because I had already spent enough money. Anyway, she had not been very nice before we had told her where we were from.

We left the store with our two packages. I found the *jinghu* player close at out heels. He introduced himself and gave us his card. He told my dad to remember to call him if we needed a troupe to come to America.

When he left, my dad pointed to his departing figure and said that was an example of what we would be treated like if we revealed our identities. We would never know if they were being nice or if they had ulterior motives.

As we were waiting for the bus, I noticed something extremely odd. The street was dark and forbidding. There were no street lights so I couldn't see anything, but I wasn't scared at all. It was eleven o'clock at night and I was standing on a dark street but I felt perfectly safe. An old lady walked past us. Her cane scratched against the sidewalk. In a city like New York, she would probably be gone by now.

It seemed weird to feel so secure on a dark street in Beijing when I would have felt extremely scared on a brightly-lit street in a large American city. Where were all of Beijing's criminals? Did they take a break at night?

When we got home, my mom took one look at the *jinghu* and didn't say anything. I could tell she thought it was a waste of time and money. I didn't care, though. I was tired enough to faint.

December 16, 1992

My dad practically dragged me out of the apartment and into the street. A taxi by the side of the road was available for us, so we jumped in and the cab sped off.

The taxi dropped us off at the corner of Wangfujing Street where we walked down the street, trying to find an instrument shop. We wanted to buy a new violin and some strings.

After walking past half of Beijing's population, we found an instrument shop. The clerks were extremely slow and we were in a bit of a hurry since it was our last day in Beijing. They didn't seem to grasp the concept of hurrying. When I asked to see the violin in the glass case behind her, she asked slowly if I wanted to see the nine hundred, the fifteen hundred, or the twenty five hundred dollar violin. I quickly chose the fifteen hundred one. She nodded and then she told me to wait while she filed her nails. It took all the willpower I possessed not to lean over and yell at her.

After she had finished filing her nails, she yelled to a person to get the violin from upstairs where they stored them. When the other person finally brought it down, I took the violin out of its fancy case. I really admired the case but I told myself that the case had nothing to do with the actual instrument. As it turned out, the instrument was terrible, so we settled for just the case.

We spent the rest of our last day in Beijing, running around, trying to see all the important sights. My dad, the photographer, must have taken 400 photos that day. Finally, we made it back to Xu Laolao's house and packed up all of our remaining belongings.

At dinner, everybody was in great spirits. We talked while we ate. It seemed like we were trying to say everything in the remaining hours. To top it all off, the dinner was delicious.

Then, my dad dragged out the camera and we all groaned. More pictures? My dad was unyielding. He dragged us all into the living room and made us smile until my jaw hurt. When he was finally done, Xu Laolao and my mom went out to find a taxi for us as we were taking the evening train to Shanghai. When they came back, they said the taxi was right outside. We packed our luggage into the taxi and said our last good-byes. As we drove off to the train station, I craned my neck this way and that to look out at Beijing one last time.

For reasons I couldn't understand, the receding sights became very important to me. Would I ever be back? Maybe but not for a long time. My eyes drank in the sights.

We were more than halfway through our trip. Would Beijing turn out to be my favorite city? Whatever the case, I would still love it for what it was: a modern and busy, yet historical and majestic capital.

December 17, 1992

Shanghai, the most populated city in China with 10.8 million people in only 6100 square km, was our next stop. I had checked on the population count even after my two Shanghainese friends had assured me of it. I just couldn't believe that Shanghai was so crowded. How was I supposed to get through Shanghai when I had hardly survived Beijing with their hordes of people.

The train trip has been long and uneventful but I don't mind so much. My thoughts keep boredom at bay. We will be seeing all kinds of famous sights and cities like the Yangtze River and Nanjing. And the whole setting on the train seems like it is right out of a story. I wish I could ride trains in the U.S., too. Riding trains is much more exciting than cars or airplanes.

In a car, I wouldn't really talk that much because I wouldn't want to distract whoever was driving. On planes, I have a history of getting nauseous. Trains seemed so natural to me. I can talk as much as I want and I don't feel the least bit sick. The only thing that bothers me is that the hole for the toilets empties straight onto the tracks. This seems a bit gross to me...

We look out the window in silence but suddenly my dad is yelling for me to look. I catch a glimpse of a river. My dad is telling me excitedly that it is the Yangtze. How I wish to climb out and stand by it. One of my friends asked me to get a rock from the Yangtze River for her but we are not stopping just yet.

Pretty soon, we were in the vicinity of Shanghai. From my window, it didn't seem very crowded. In fact, it looked like a small village. Was this supposed to be Shanghai?

The train stopped. I felt my first bit of uncertainty. What

in the world would happen during my stay here? Would the people like us or dislike us? What would Shanghai be like? Would it really be crowded?

I was given charge over a little suitcase and a backpack. I got both off the train and waited as my parents struggled with the other four. When my parents finally stepped off the train, they both looked exhausted.

One man came over to us and offered to take our luggage on his cart. By now, almost everybody had already left the platform so we accepted his help.

He told us that the station was pretty far from the platform so we would have to go across the railroad tracks. At first, I kind of doubted his word because I thought the architects would have the sense to put the station near the platform.

As we crossed the railroad tracks, I shivered. I wondered how much waste was under my feet. After all, people did use the bathroom on the train.

We hopped in a taxi and drove away from the station. My first glance at Shanghai gave me a heart attack. People, cars and buses were all crowded on the streets. It was worse than Beijing and Guangzhou put together.

The streets were crowded with cars and buses. The traffic was just as bad. It seemed to take us hours to get to the hotel.

When my dad got out of the hotel shower, he decided to make a phone call to his cousin who lived in Shanghai. We had promised him that we would pay him a visit. By this time, my stomach was starting to growl and so was my dad's, so he said we'd stop by after we ate some dinner.

My mom had a headache so we left her in the room. Outside the hotel, everything was pitch black so we decided to walk along the street until we found a restaurant. Before long, I spotted a nice-looking restaurant. The lights were still twinkling so we crossed the street and entered.

We were seated by the window and then the waitress

handed us the menus. Both my dad and I almost jumped out of our skins. The prices were a lot more expensive than we had expected.

That was when my dad and I saw the big TV and the two little ones at the far end of the restaurant. No wonder it was so expensive. We had just walked straight into a Karaoke bar! As I found out, Karaoke was all the rage in China and all the young people were doing it.

When we realized what type of restaurant we were in, my dad told the waitress we wanted to sit in the center, where we could be closer to the TV.

I left the ordering up to my dad. He started spewing out names of dishes as she furiously wrote. When he was finished, we settled back and enjoyed the music.

The waitress kept bringing more and more food. One dish was very unusual. She brought over a pot full of oil, a stove and a plate that had octopus and other things on it. She set it all on our table and put the pot on the stove.

She tossed the raw food into the oil and cooked our meal right in front of us. This was the first time I had experienced anything like this.

During the course of our meal some men had come in. At first, I didn't really notice them but later they started singing and I listened to them. It wasn't their singing that attracted my attention, though.

They complimented the waitresses and asked the waitresses to sing some songs. They drank wine, and even offered a waitress wine out of his cup. This didn't surprise me but my dad observed that this kind of behavior would have been extremely shameful a few years ago.

I didn't want to sing because I have a horrible singing voice and I couldn't read the Chinese words fast enough to sing them. They had songs in English but I didn't know most of them. Anyway, singing in English didn't make any difference since I would still be tone deaf.

After dinner we went to meet my dad's cousin. Upon arriving at his apartment, my dad got warm welcomes and I was introduced. I immediately liked his wife, but their sons were so quiet I couldn't really judge them.

I found out that the couple both went to Qinghua University in Beijing which is one of the best universities in China. But even so, they weren't faring very well. Together, they were only earning five hundred *yuan* (approximately $70.00 U.S.) a month.

To me, that seemed unfair. They were graduates of Qinghua University, but their whole family had to live on five hundred *yuan* a month while taxi drivers, who hardly had an education at all, earned more than a thousand a month.

Everybody was starting to get tired so my dad suggested that we go home. Before we left, though, he gave them some presents. My dad's cousin wouldn't take them. It took them about twenty minutes to finish arguing about the presents. In the end, they accepted everything except the money.

"We were brought up together, and I haven't sunk that low yet. We can not take your money," they told us.

They were both proud and respectful people. We had to leave so we had to accept their decision of not accepting the money. My dad said that was just normal Chinese custom.

I think arguing about presents is a waste of time. The giver wants the receiver to be happy and enjoy them. Receiving presents does not mean you are less of a human than the giver. The time they wasted might as well have been used for talking or saying decent goodbyes. The Chinese have not figured that out yet.

We got into our taxi and sped off back to the hotel.

December 18, 1992

My parents had planned to take me to do some shopping today. They decided on Nanjing Road because it was supposed to be the best place to shop in China.

The hotel doorman opened the door and the warm air bathed my face. It was definitely a change from Beijing's freezing climate. The streets seemed perpetually crowded with cars and people.

We took the bus to Nanjing Road and started walking. When I first saw it, I had to draw in a few breaths and look again. The street was crowded with people, people and more people.

There were stores on both sides of the street: department stores, shoe stores, designer clothes stores and men's clothing stores. There had to be more than one thousand stores on this street!

My lips were ten inches apart. I just stared and pointed. These stores weren't just normal stores. They were some of the fanciest and most expensive ones in Shanghai.

After my astonishment had simmered, we continued on our way. My dad was very amused by my reaction. He asked me if I had really thought that China was so unsophisticated.

We walked uncomfortably down the street with people pushing and bumping into us, stopping to look at some things. We were planning to walk to the bridge at the other end of the street where all the department stores were.

We didn't get there.

I was so awed by a display of a dress that I stopped in my tracks and stared. It was perfect. I couldn't take my eyes off it. My parents saw my amazement and they finally gave way and let me go in the store.

Inside the store, two saleswomen came over to help.

One of them ushered me into a fitting room but I didn't start changing immediately. The lady just stood there. She stared at me while I stared back. After a while, I realized she wasn't planning on leaving, so I started changing. She quickly rushed to my side to help me change.

Before I was finished changing, she started staring at me. She looked at me like I was crazy. "Is anything wrong?" I asked.

She shook her head slowly and replied, "You're going to freeze to death."

Now that was surprising. What in the world did she mean by that?

She explained by saying, "Shouldn't you have on more than one shirt?"

This time, I stared at her like she was crazy. Shanghai was definitely not Beijing. If the weather was as cold as Beijing, I would probably put on more than one shirt, but in Shanghai?

We came out of the fitting room. While my parents were admiring the dress, the lady started bugging my mom about how I was bound to catch a cold. Finally, my mom told her that we lived in the U.S.

For some reason, the word "U.S." is sacred in China. Both salesladies were immediately nicer than before. They even tried to interest my mom and dad in some clothes. When we eventually left the store, both ladies accompanied us to the door and told us in some very pleasant tones that they would always welcome us back in their store.

The brisk afternoon air greeted us. Leaving the store, we were once again confronted with people but by now we were used to it. I didn't feel so uncomfortable anymore. We walked on and on. Soon, I saw a huge bridge and two stores above it.

At first, when I read the name of the bigger store, I was a little confused. It said Number Ten Department Store on it. A Number Ten Department Store? What in the world did the Number Ten mean? While I was still puzzling over it, my parents explained to me that we had walked this far to see this store.

I was stumped. All that walking for this? I must have shown my disappointment because my parents immediately explained that this department store sold just about everything you could possibly hope for.

Everything I could ask for? I could think of a lot of things they probably didn't sell. As we walked onto the bridge, I listened to some information about this store. It used to be the biggest department store in Shanghai in the 1930's and 40's. You could find anything you wished for in this store. Today, the Number One Department Store, which we were going to, was supposedly bigger and had a wider variety of things.

We were in the middle of the bridge when I realized I had lost sight of my parents. I couldn't hear their voices, nor could I see them. The crowds around me intensified, and I felt very uncomfortable. There were even more people on the bridge than on the street.

Someone caught onto my coat. I stopped and stood still. People around me started complaining and pushing when I stopped but I didn't care. I closed my eyes and waited for a blade to cut through me.

When I turned around, though, I saw my mom. I was so relieved I almost fainted but she prevented that by pulling me up straighter. We walked close to each other and tried to make our way through the mess. As we got closer and closer to the center, the crowd got tighter and tighter around us. It was so crowded that when I looked down, I couldn't tell my own feet apart from the other people's.

After checking out the entire department store, I was really tired, but we hadn't seen a bookstore yet. The nearest one would be a huge bookstore on Fuzhou Street.

I laughed since Fuzhou was my hometown and bookstores are like a second home to me. What a coincidence! It was also the town we were going to the next day.

My dad explained that in Shanghai, all the streets in this area were named after cities in China. For example, Nanjing

Road was named for the city Nanjing.

We soon arrived at the bookstore. I went in and asked a clerk where the foreign language section was. It turned out to be on the third floor so we walked up the stairs. At the entrance to the third floor, there was a little barrier keeping us from going in. An old man hobbled over.

He asked in Chinese, "Foreigner or Chinese?"

Before I could answer, my dad replied, "Foreigner."

He poked me in the side when I tried to say that we were Chinese. I got the point but I had no earthly idea why I was supposed to keep quiet. The man looked at us suspiciously and then let us in.

My dad finally explained after we had buried ourselves in a quiet corner, "He wouldn't have let us in if we had said we were Chinese."

"But why?" I asked.

"Because they have some books in this section that some Chinese would object to."

"Like what?"

Unfortunately, my dad couldn't give me an answer to that question. What a strange policy. Didn't they want to sell books?

After we paid for everything, we left the store and walked along the road. While we were walking, my dad got another crazy idea.

"Why don't we go walk along the waterfront? It's really near here," he said.

First, in Guangzhou, we had to see the Zhu River (Pearl River); on the train, we had to see the Yangtze River; now we had to take a walk along Huangpu River.

At first, my mom and I were hesitant but we were quickly persuaded that it would be a good experience for me to see the river. We walked down the street and took a right on a street called Zhongshan Road East.

Down the street, a huge building loomed over us.

"Do you feel like going in?" my dad asked us.

"Not really. Why? Do you want to?" my mom answered.

"Remember, we need another suitcase. One of ours is about to fall apart and now we have so many souvenirs that there won't be enough space in the suitcases."

My mom agreed.

The store was very big. It was also very empty. Only clerks stood there and they looked half asleep. All the suitcases were on display in a glass case so we took a look at them.

A woman with a sleepy expression walked out.

"Need help?" she asked.

"We would like to look at that suitcase, please."

She went inside and brought out one exactly like it. My dad started examining it carefully and adding pressure to it but it seemed okay so we bought the suitcase. After buying it, we were on the verge of leaving when a woman rushed over to us.

"Hello, would you like to buy a suit?" she asked, addressing my dad.

"No," he replied bluntly.

This didn't seem to put her off.

"We have some nice fabric that I'm sure would suit you. We also have some very nice colors," she said, trying to entice my dad.

I looked over to where she was pointing. I had not noticed the suits being displayed in the corner. Somehow the woman managed to drag us over to the racks. She pulled out a few suits that looked alright but we really didn't have the time to buy another suit, nor the money. Finally, she convinced my dad to try on a suit that would fit him the best.

My dad disappeared into the fitting room, which was actually the restroom. While he was in there, the saleswoman started talking. Her mind seemed to be filled with thousands of things to talk about. Then she focused on my clothes.

"Oh my God, you only have one shirt on!"

What was wrong with these people? I quickly told her that I wasn't cold but she continued to shake her head.

When my dad finally came out, she shifted her attention to him. The suit looked okay. There were a few bad points but my dad listed them before I could even open my mouth.

The saleswoman had a lively mouth and she came up with two good points for every bad one. My dad couldn't outtalk her. I wondered if the Shanghai salespeople got training on how to talk. One thing was for sure: they could teach Beijing salespeople how to do business.

In the end, my dad did buy the suit, mostly to make the woman shut up. While the woman was bagging the suit, she asked us where we were from.

Without hesitating, my dad answered, "America."

She was surprised, but quick to react.

"Will you take my daughter with you?" she asked jokingly. "Then, your daughter will have an older sister."

At first, I was surprised by this question but my dad just laughed. After we left the store, my parents gave sighs of relief.

Then, my dad pointed to the street in front of us.

"Behind that street is Huangpu River. Come on!"

Both my mom and I followed my dad. He was right. We walked past the wide avenue and came to some steps. We climbed up and I caught my first glimpse of the Huangpu River.

There was nothing spectacular about it. It was just a muddy river but according to my dad, the Huangpu River is one of the biggest ports in China. It stretched 35 miles and brought many imports to Shanghai.

The wind was starting to become very strong. The waves slammed against the wall and against me until I was soaked with water. We moved away from the wall and climbed down the stairs. My dad flagged a taxi and all three of us climbed in.

December 19, 1992

I could hardly contain my excitement.

I couldn't believe I was actually going to see my grandmother and all my other relatives. I loved to hear my friends talk about their family reunions, and I had always wished to go to one myself. That wouldn't have been possible unless we had gone back to China.

Now, I would go to my first one. I couldn't wait. During the taxi ride to Hongqiao Airport, my mind was concentrating on Fuzhou and everybody I would see. I didn't even notice the empty streets around me.

My mom was the first to comment, "This sure is different from yesterday."

"What?" I asked, coming out of my reverie.

"The traffic," she pointed out.

I looked outside. She was right. There were hardly any cars. We were just cruising along with no difficulty. My dad had been wrong. He had assumed we would get in a traffic jam so he had asked the taxi to come two hours earlier than our flight time.

Within minutes, we were at the airport.

The airport seemed very nice. The waiting rooms were clean and large but my whole image of the airport was very blurry. For some reason, the other airports seemed very different from this one. Hongqiao Airport didn't seem crowded like the other ones. There wasn't a single sound. It was also much cleaner than the other airports in China. It reminded me of a hospital because it was so white and silent.

At about eight o'clock, we boarded the plane, and after take-off, I immediately fell asleep.

"Hey!" the man behind us cried. "Are you from Fuzhou?"

My eyes popped open and I turned around. A guy had

stuck his head between my dad's seat and my window seat. Before my parents could get out a word, he started talking again.

"I heard you two speaking in Fuzhounese," he explained, this time in Fuzhou dialect.

"Yes," my dad answered.

The man stuck his hand out and shook my dad's.

"I live in Japan. What about you?"

"We live in the United States," my mom replied.

"Oh. What do you do?" he asked.

My dad said, "I work in a university."

"Professor?"

"No."

"Well, I'm a snakehead."

I couldn't restrain myself.

"You're a what?"

"A snakehead," he answered confidently.

My dad nudged me and I closed my mouth which at that moment was wide open. I had an idea what a snakehead was but I wasn't sure about it. Later, my parents explained that it was a slang term the Chinese use for a person who arranges for illegal immigrants to sneak into to a country. Many snakeheads work in America, Japan and a few of the European countries. In return, the illegal immigrants pay the snakeheads. Usually, the price is between twenty thousand to one hundred thousand dollars.

The man continued his talk about how great he was and how easy it was to earn money in his profession. In fact, the trip to Fuzhou was to pick up another one of his customers. I couldn't believe he was actually telling us all this. Why was he not afraid that we would turn him in?

My eyes strayed to my watch. I almost jumped out of my seat. Twenty more minutes until we landed. I wanted to burst with joy. My parents obviously felt the same. I could tell by the way they were eagerly looking out the window.

When we got off the plane, we ran as fast as we could

toward the terminal. I could already envision our reunion.

At the baggage pick-up area, I looked around but no one was in sight except the people on our flight. My dad rushed off to find my grandmother and Mr. Zhu, who were picking us up.

My mom and I were frustrated so we went back into the terminal building to wait. I started getting restless so I asked my mom if I could go out for a breath of fresh air. When I left the building, I blinked a few times and stared at the two people coming toward me.

With a cry of delight, I ran into my grandmother's arms. It felt so good to be near her again. I squeezed my eyes shut and pinched myself. It wasn't a dream.

After our very prolonged hug, I gave the woman standing beside me a questioning look. It was my great-aunt! While I was talking to her, I heard footsteps behind me. A pair of arms circled my grandmother.

It was my dad, followed by my mom and Mr. Zhu, whom I didn't recognize at first. After all the greetings had gone around, my dad went off ahead with Mr. Zhu, leaving my mom, my grandmother, my great-aunt and me alone. We walked leisurely, taking our time and talking.

In front of the terminal, we came face to face with a man on a bicycle.

He was ringing a bell and calling, "Fish balls! Come and buy some fish balls!"

The smell that wafted into my nose stopped me. My mom looked at me and started laughing. She stopped the man and asked him to get me a bowl of fish balls. The man got off his bike and opened the container holding the soup. On the other side of the container was a rack where he kept all the salts and spices.

Fish balls are made of fish, tapioca, salt and meat. These are the most basic ingredients. Many stores add other things to make it taste better but in Fuzhou, fish balls are usually made with very secret recipes.

The man started dishing out the fish balls. He put them in

soup and passed the bowl over to me. I dug my teeth into the first one. It immediately brought back memories of the first time I had fish balls in a restaurant.

That was when I was almost four. My grandfather was the person that took me. I remember I had just gotten over being sick and my grandfather and I wanted to give my grandmother a surprise...

We took a bus over to the company she worked in to visit her. When she saw me, she immediately started scolding the two of us. After a while, she made my grandfather take me home but he didn't follow her directions.

When we were outside, he asked me if I liked fish balls. I wasn't sure what they were at the time but at that age, you say yes to anything so I nodded. He took my hand and we walked and walked.

Soon, we arrived at a little restaurant. We sat down at a table in front of the restaurant because we wanted to eat outside.

My grandfather said to me, "Okay, today, you're going to have some fish balls."

I nodded my head excitedly although I had no idea what fish balls were. My grandfather ordered a bowl for me. I remember when I first bit into the fish ball, I was so surprised at the taste I almost dropped it. The soup was hot so my grandfather had to blow on it. In the end, we shared the bowl, and that is how my love for fish balls began.

This time, although the soup was hot, nobody was there to blow on it. That memory immediately triggered another one that I had not thought about for a long time...

The Chinese often take naps after lunch so it was no surprise that my grandfather wanted to sleep one Saturday afternoon. Unfortunately, he wanted me to do so, too. He had spent most of the morning playing with me so he was tired out. I was only three years old, and most three-year-olds can-

not sleep after playing so hard. However, he forced me to lie down. Before I knew it, my grandfather was snoring.

At that time, I could have easily snuck out but I didn't want to. I knew Nai-nai (grandmother) wouldn't play with me and neither of my parents was there. Anyway, I loved to play with my grandfather. He was the most fun, and he told jokes like no other person.

I racked my brain for an answer. My grandfather was snoring hard enough to wake the dead so I knew I couldn't easily wake him. Finally, I came up with a plan.

I crawled softly off the bed. First, I reached for my grandfather's glasses. I gently lifted them off his face and placed them in a drawer in the end table. Then, I ran around to the foot of the bed, where his feet were. I began to tickle his feet with both hands.

He immediately started howling. I hurriedly ran to the door and hid behind it.

Seconds later, he was yelling, "Where are my glasses? Where are my glasses?"

I couldn't hold in my laughter. A few minutes later, Nai-nai exposed me, and they both took turns scolding me, but it was worth it. The look on my grandfather's face was enough for me...

I came out of my reverie as I finished my first bowl. Then, my mom bought me another one. I gulped it down in a very short time, but my grandmother put a restraining arm on my shoulder. She wouldn't let me eat any more.

The truck that my great aunt had driven to pick us up was pretty large so it could have fit us all, but my grandmother was adamant about not getting on it. She had come in a bicycle rickshaw and planned to go home in one, too. She had even asked the man that had brought her to wait outside.

My parents decided to let me go with my grandmother.

The airport was a good distance away from where my grandmother lived, so we were able to relax. As we slowly rode along, all I could catch sight of were rows of crops and workers in the fields wearing big, shady hats.

After a short while, we crossed over a huge bridge. I looked down at the rippling waters of the Min River. My grandmother told me that we were now in the "city."

We rode through a good number of streets, and the crowds seemed to get larger and larger. The streets were filled with cars, bicycles, bicycle rickshaws, and people.

The rickshaw stopped at the most crowded street I had seen so far. "We are home," she said.

We walked up the stairs to the third floor where my grandmother's apartment was. The door was open, so we walked straight in.

My parents and Mr. Zhu were standing in the middle of the room. Our suitcases and boxes had been stacked against the wall. The room was quiet. I followed my mom's gaze and it led me to a picture of my grandfather.

In China, when a person in the family dies, the person's picture is usually hung up in the center of the wall. My grandmother and I stared solemnly at the picture. Tears started forming at the corners of her eyes. Mr. Zhu soon left, seeing that we wanted to be alone.

My grandmother started telling us the story of my grandfather's death.

"One day, after I got back from my visit to America, I went to the hairdresser. It was one of the rare occasions when I left the house," she started off. "The people from the bank where he worked arrived after I left. When they got up here, they heard a yell from upstairs. They rushed up and found him half kneeling on the floor."

With a pause, she continued, "They, they called the ambulance and then came to get me. When we got to the hospital, he was taken into the emergency room. It seemed like ages before the doctor told us he had a stroke. He was in a coma. They waited a few hours before taking him into surgery.

"It didn't really help. He was still in the coma. They gave

him his room and tried to think of ways to help him. After the doctor came out of the surgery room, I secretly gave him a few hundred *yuan*. I hoped he might try harder to help him."

"Isn't that a bribe? But you could get in trouble for that," I mumbled.

My dad shot me a warning glance and I immediately got quiet.

"The doctor said that an acupuncturist might be able to help, so I took him to the acupuncturist. I also gave him some money. He took it, but he wasn't able to help him, either. Nobody could help him," she explained with a sob.

"At first, whenever anybody touched him, he could move a little bit. After a while, he had no response at all. It was almost as if he was dead. After two months passed, the doctor told me I could take him home. There was nothing they could do for him."

She stopped and sighed.

"I went to the job agency and put up an ad for nurses. Two came. I paid each two hundred sixty *yuan* a month. Since his brain couldn't work, he couldn't eat or get rid of his wastes. The two nurses helped me. However, they only stayed for two weeks."

"Next, I hired a young man for five hundred *yuan* a month. He stayed for a little longer. One day, I went out to buy some food. When I got back, the room was locked. Usually, the door is never locked. I got out my key and went in. The man was gone but your father was still there. A stereo system you gave him was gone, and a few hundred *yuan* was gone," she told us.

"I think the man figured that your father was about to die so the job wasn't about to last. A few days later, your father was red in the face, and he couldn't breathe very well. I called all his brothers and sisters, and they came. I also called long distance to my sister and brother-in-law. They came all the way from Lanping on a train."

By this time, we could barely hear her; she was so distraught with the painful memories.

"They arrived about half an hour earlier. We all stood there and watched him. He was very lucky that all his brothers and sisters were there. But I don't think he realized it. Thirty minutes later, he was gone."

My grandmother broke out into sobs. My father also had tears rolling down his cheeks. My great-aunt was sitting on a chair. She was staring at the ground.

A few minutes later, my grandmother continued, "I sent the fax to you the day after because I didn't want you to rush back to China."

She didn't know that my dad had tried to do that. The minute he got the fax he called the airport and asked if there were any planes heading for China. All the planes had already left that morning. He would have to wait another day for another airplane. By then, it would have been too late to attend the funeral.

"There was a big problem at first. There was nobody to carry the picture of your father since you were in the United States," my grandmother told my dad.

In China, when somebody dies, his or her son usually sat on the hearse and held a picture of the deceased.

"Well, I wanted to ask your cousin to do it, but one of the relatives cut in. She said that whoever held the picture also got the family's possessions. At first, I was extremely angry. She was just jealous," she concluded.

My grandmother loved us very much, and she had always dreamed that we would come back to China to live. She thought that a family should always be together. That was why she wanted to leave the apartment we bought for her to us. She was hoping that we might come back someday to live in China.

"Well? Who held the picture in the end?" I asked.

"Me."

Everybody was quiet. I didn't want to break the silence, so I lay down on the bed.

Sounds coming from the kitchen started getting louder and louder. I opened one eyelid. Where was everybody? I jumped out of bed and checked in the kitchen. My grandmother was in there fixing dinner. I looked at her closely. There were still traces of tears on her face, but other than that, she looked okay. "Your dad went out and your mom is upstairs with your aunt," she answered when I asked about my parents.

My dad came bounding in with a small plastic bag. I took it from him and peeked inside.

Before I even saw what it was, I smelled it. It had to be fish balls! Now, where in the world had my dad gone to buy them?

My grandmother bopped my dad on the head and asked, "Still have that old craving for fish balls, huh?"

She went back into the kitchen and left my dad and me staring at a long bench at the table.

He pointed to the bench and asked me, "Do you remember the story I told you about that bench?"

"No, why?"

"I'll tell you now. When I was a kid, my parents weren't as lenient with me as I am with you. I got in trouble for the tiniest mistake. Well, one day, I got into trouble but I don't really remember what for. My punishment was that I had to be tied to this bench," he began.

"They tied you to a bench?" I asked incredulously.

"Yes," he answered. "I screamed and yelled and cried but nobody came to my rescue. I was miserable. However, while I screamed and yelled and cried, I was also moving around a whole lot and the ropes weren't very tight. Soon, the ropes fell to the ground."

"What did you do? Run away?" I suggested.

"Nope. I started screaming 'Help, the ropes came loose! The ropes came loose!'"

I burst out laughing.

"How old were you?"

"I can't remember, but I know I was very little."

I couldn't stop laughing.

"Well, did she retie you?" I asked.

"No, she started laughing so hard she couldn't even tie me up again," he explained.

At that moment, my mother, a woman and her daughter appeared in the doorway. I found out the woman was my Aunt Guo Fang. I looked at the little girl. Who was this adorable girl? It surely couldn't be my cousin Yang Se because this girl in no way resembled the chubby little girl in the pictures.

After a lot of staring, my aunt introduced us. It was indeed my cousin. Not only had her looks changed dramatically but also her attitude. My aunt had written how naughty and rude Yang Se had been. Now, she still had a childish air but seemed very well-behaved in front of others.

Only a few minutes after we were introduced, we became friends. Dinner was served, and everyone sat down around the rickety table. The food was absolutely wonderful, and the fish ball soup was great.

The dinner took us about an hour because we talked while we ate. My aunt wanted to know everything that had happened during the years. She also talked about her upcoming divorce. That was the bitter part of the meal.

Once we started on this topic, my grandmother immediately excused Yang Se and me from the table. What was the big deal? A lot of my friends' parents were divorced. It wasn't a forbidden topic. However, in China, it was, and we had to leave the table.

Yang Se and I went back into the room and flipped on the TV. My grandmother didn't have a lot of channels, but I flipped through the ones she had.

Yang Se and I watched television for awhile, but soon I had to use the restroom. I was having problems locating it, so I went back into the living room and asked, "Mom, where's the restroom?"

"Oh, the chamberpot is at the foot of the stairs," she answered.

"The what?" I yelled.

"The foot of the stairs," she repeated, not understanding what I meant.

"Mom, I'm talking about that other word, or did I just imagine it?" I demanded.

"Are you talking about the chamberpot?" she asked.

"Of course!"

"What about it?"

"What about it? I have never in my life used a chamberpot, and I don't plan to," I explained.

"Well, you can always wait until tomorrow," she suggested.

"But I can't," I told her miserably.

In the end, I was convinced to use it. My mom handed me some tissues and I hurried off to get it over with. When I was done, though, I had a problem. Where was I supposed to dump it?

"Just leave it there," she said.

I couldn't be happier to oblige. What a family reunion this had been! I was exhausted and in need of some serious rest.

December 20, 1992

Somebody was staring at me. I could feel dark eyes penetrating through my skull. I shifted uncomfortably but I still had that weird feeling. I opened my eyes slowly. I was facing my grandmother.

Relieved that it was just Nai-nai, I closed my eyes again. Nai-nai is the Chinese word for grandmother. Soon, though, I felt the eyes staring at me again. I could feel the person staring at the back of my head. I turned my head abruptly, making my cousin jump.

"Gosh, you are so lazy," she complained. "It's six-thirty already! I was wondering when you would finally wake up."

I looked at the girl through slanted eyelids. Was she going crazy, or was I going deaf?

"Excuse me?" I mumbled, certain that I had heard wrong.

"I said you should be awake already. It's six-thirty!" she repeated.

I was fully awake by this time.

"Six-thirty!"

"I knew you would be ashamed of yourself!" she scolded.

How could I have ever thought this girl was cute? She obviously belonged in an asylum for psychotic patients. I ignored her and turned over. My grandmother started to help her.

"Get up!" she ordered, much to my despair.

Correct the statement before. Both my grandmother and my cousin were loonies. Getting up at six-thirty on a day when there was no school? Nine o'clock would be early enough for me!

"I do not plan to get up at six-thirty in the morning when I could be resting my tired body," I retorted.

"Why?" she asked, seeing no reason. "What's the matter with six-thirty?"

My grandparents and I—picture taken five months before I came to the United States.

When I first came here, I was such a little thing.

Receiving a scholarship from the Center for Talented Youth—The Johns Hopkins University.

Bobo and I.

I took out my laptop and started writing my diary on the airplane.

Hong Kong: We stepped onto a noisy street.

What we saw outside was another type of Hong Kong.

Guanzhou Train Station.

The sight of the snakes was amusing until my dad informed me that we were having them for lunch.

My parents and I at Sun Yat-sen Memorial.

Guangzhou: Mausoleum of 72 Martyrs at Huanghuagang in memory of the "March 29 Campaign" of the Revolution of 1911.

Yihe Yuan (Summer Palace).

Ruins at Yuanming Yuan.

Tiananmen and View from Tiananmen Terrace.

I tried to imagine what it would feel like if I were Chairman Mao up there.

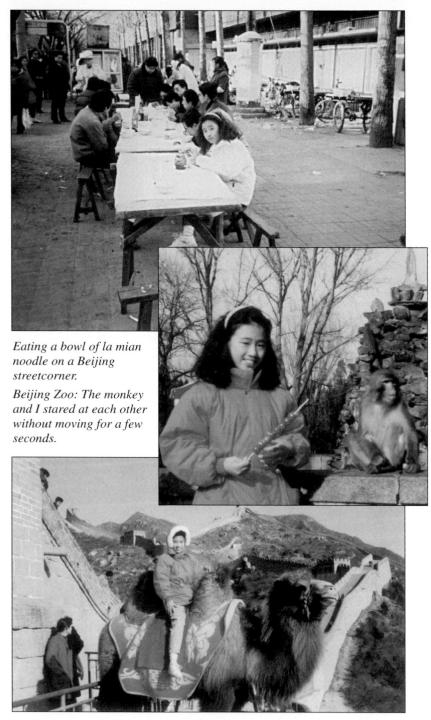

Eating a bowl of la mian noodle on a Beijing streetcorner.

Beijing Zoo: The monkey and I stared at each other without moving for a few seconds.

I climbed the Great Wall.

On the train to Shanghai:
we sat at the tables beside
the compartments.

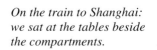

Shanghai: It was so crowded, I couldn't
tell my own feet apart from the other
people's.

Shanghai: Nanjing Street.

Biking in Fuzhou.

Fuzhou:
Ancient Street.

Fuzhou: Xihu Park (West Lake Park).

Fuzhou: Reconstruction City.

Fuzhou: Biking in front of our new apartment where my grandmother now lives.

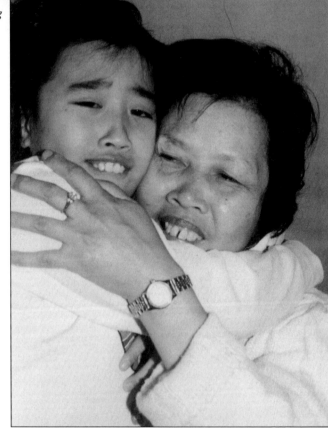

Our farewells were extremely depressing.

"Why?" I practically yelled.

Then, I remembered. My dad told me that Chinese children got up at six-thirty every single day. The minute I remembered I felt bad for being mad at my cousin. My dad had told me this one morning when I wouldn't get up.

Chinese children attended school at eight o'clock just like the Texans but instead of lazing in bed, they got up at around five-thirty to six. These two hours weren't used to spray their hair or play Nintendo. The children in China got up in the morning to study. The two hours were devoted to memorizing the textbook.

The children wouldn't just look at it. They would read it out loud.

One of the questions I had was, why in the world did they not memorize everything the night before? Had they been outside playing? My dad could only laugh at that question. I found out the children had so much homework they couldn't fit everything in at night. Also, Chinese people believed that morning is the best time to memorize things.

Finally, I let my cousin pull me out of bed. Anyway, by then, I was pretty much wide awake.

My grandmother cooked breakfast and soon, we were all assembled around the table. Breakfast consisted of gruel with different types of relishes.

My mom brought up the subject of going to her mother's house, and said that my other grandmother on my mom's side, or Wai-po, would invite a lot of relatives and have a small family reunion. When I heard this, I couldn't wait to leave.

My grandmother began bustling around, dusting and sweeping. My mom said she was going to make a phone call and went for the front door.

"So, where's the phone?"

"We don't have our personal phone. I go downstairs whenever I need to use one," she explained.

With my eyes as large as saucers, I exclaimed, "Stop pull-

ing my leg! You'll never fool me! No phone? Impossible!
How can someone not have a phone"

My grandmother just smiled and went on sweeping. Finally, the knowledge sank to my brain. No phone.

"Okay, okay. Where is it?"

"Go down the stairs and you'll see it right before you go
out the gate. It's in a little room," she replied, still smiling.

I walked down with my cousin. To my relief, she told me
she had a phone. At least one member of this society wasn't
suffering from phone deprivation. We decided to take a bicycle rickshaw since it was fun to ride in.

*Fuzhou had changed so much from what it used to be. My
dad noticed it right away, but I was only slowly realizing.
What had happened to the quiet, little streets we used to fre-
quent?*

*Bicycles and cars zoomed around. Unlike the other cit-
ies, Fuzhou wasn't dominated by buses. The majority of the
vehicles seemed to be bicycle rickshaws.*

We knocked on the door, which immediately swung open
and a wrinkled face peeked out at us. With a scream, my
cousin opened the screen door and nearly clobbered Wai-po.
Wai-po opened the door wider, and another wrinkled face
appeared. It was another one of my numerous aunts.

Both women welcomed us joyously.

Soon after, I met my other younger cousin, Zhang Jing.
He was a very intelligent young man who acted as big brother
for Yang Se. When we came to the kitchen, I saw another
woman. She was introduced as my second youngest aunt,
Aunt Guo Su.

She was busy cooking something, but she wouldn't let
me see what it was. Judging by the aroma it had to be something delicious. The four of us just stood there for a while
but soon she urged us to go outside and play.

After running around for awhile, I soon grew weary and
decided to go back inside. Wai-po was setting the table. The

others were all in the kitchen. Soon, the dishes started appearing on the table. The delicious aroma washed away every idea except eating. Within minutes, we all sat down and were ravenously grabbing at the food.

After lunch, we all went out to the living room to talk.

"So, when you go to school, what is it like?" my uncle asked, directing the question at both my mom and me.

I answered, "Oh, I usually wake up around seven. The school bus picks me up at seven-thirty. I have breakfast at school, and then I go to class. After my fourth class, I have lunch. Then, I have three more classes in the afternoon."

"How long are they?" one of my aunts asked.

Before I could answer, another aunt asked, "How much do you pay for breakfast and lunch? Is it free? Is it expensive?"

The questions were shot at us so fast, we could hardly answer but my mom and I took one question at a time. The questions were also very bizarre. One person even wanted to know what color school buses were.

"I have seven classes in all, plus an advisory. Advisory is just where you can learn about the "good" things in life. Each class is forty five minutes long with a five minute break in between. School starts at eight fifteen and ends at three fifteen," I answered.

My mom answered the other question, "At first, it was free since our income was below a certain level but then it raised to forty cents and then to seventy and now it is a dollar twenty five."

"What classes do you have?"

By this time, I had given up trying to keep up with who had asked what.

"I have language, arts, advanced math, science, advanced orchestra, physical education, social studies and a gifted and talented class."

"What is orchestra? What is gifted and talented?"

"Well, our school has an orchestra and I'm in it. We're a

fairly good orchestra, too. Gifted and talented is a class for the gifted and talented. Basically, we just do projects that involve higher thinking skills."

"Wow, so you must be really smart!" someone exclaimed. "How did you get in the class? Is it hard?"

"She got in by taking some tests," my mom answered.

"It's not exactly hard but sometimes it is challenging," I said in answer to the second question.

"Are the teachers very strict?"

"No, not at all. You just have to follow the rules, which are just basic manners," I replied.

Yang Se and Zhang Jing had appeared in the doorway.

"They're that easy on you?" Yang Se asked. "At my school, everybody has to follow all of the teacher's instructions. Everybody must respect the teachers."

"Yes, they're pretty easy on us. They do things to help us study better, even if it ruins their image. In a school near ours, the principal jumped into a Jacuzzi full of chocolate because the students all passed a test. He had a suit on so his suit was ruined, and he got a chocolate bath," I told them.

"He really jumped in? With his suit on?" Aunt Guo Fang sputtered.

"Yes. Another time, we had a fundraiser selling candy. My orchestra teachers said that anybody who sold seventy five items or more could shove a pie into their faces. One of my friends sold that many. She shoved the pie into my teacher's face, and then she even pushed it up into her nose. My teacher was standing there with pie up her nose."

"Did she get mad?" Wai-po asked.

"No, of course not! She just laughed," I explained.

"You have a strange teacher with a strange sense of humor," my uncle told me.

"This is the funniest story. Every year, there is a Kiss the Pig contest at my school. It's a fundraiser. Milk cartons are put in the library. Every milk carton has a different teacher's name on it. Students can go to the library and put money in the cartons. At the end of the contest, the teacher who has the most money in their can has to kiss a pig."

"Why would the kids waste their money?" one of my aunts asked.

"Because they want to see the teachers humiliated," I explained.

My relatives started mumbling among themselves. I could tell they thought Americans were really weird.

"Is Texas hot? Where do you live?" asked a cousin.

"Yes, Texas is hot but not as hot as Fuzhou."

A nod from one of my cousins set her on a roll again. " The big difference is you don't notice the temperature much in Texas because you're usually inside with the air conditioner on."

I decided I was going to steal the show from my mom, and I did.

I answered the second question by saying, "We live in College Station. It is a medium sized city with around sixty thousand people. It's called College Station because it has a university in the middle of it. Most people living there are students and faculty. Texas A&M is one of the largest universities in the U.S. When it was first founded, it was called Texas Agriculture and Mechanics. That is what A&M stands for."

"Do you fit in there?"

"Pretty much. We understand everything they do, and we know how to act on different occasions. Let me assure you, it is very different from China," my mom answered in a rush.

"Do you like living there?"

"Yes," I answered.

"Kind of," my mom replied.

The questions went on and on. There were questions from what kind of lifestyle we had to what kind of soap we used. They were so eager to find out more about America. So many people had given them wonderful accounts of America. In Chinese, America is called *mei guo. Mei* means beautiful and *guo* means country, so it means "beautiful country".

Yang Se started nodding off. Her mother noticed and made

her go into a little bedroom to sleep. My aunts must have noticed my yawns because soon, I was also ushered into the bedroom by the kitchen.

When I woke up, everyone was still outside, and my mom was still talking. What in the world was so interesting about what my mom was saying? They acted like my mom was a goddess bringing home information from the heavens.

Wai-po held up a bag of sunflower seeds and motioned for me to sit down. I declined by saying that I needed some exercise.

Pretty soon, Yang Se appeared on the scene with Zhang Jing, and we all raced outside. Zhang Jing began attacking Yang Se. They looked like they were playing tag. Zhang Jing was screaming for me to hold Yang Se, and she was screaming for me to help her. I decided to help neither one but to watch instead.

Then I got the idea to attack both of them. I approached the two with my tickling fingers ready. Both saw me coming. At first, they thought I was going to help them but when I started tickling them, they started screaming even louder. Yang Se seemed to be very ticklish. Zhang Jing was ticklish too, but he didn't scream every time I poked him in the stomach like Yang Se did.

Unfortunately, I didn't know that Yang Se and Zhang Jing were both advanced ticklers, too. Somehow, they exchanged a silent message, and then I became the screaming lunatic. Why did I think I could out-tickle them?

Soon, I was sick to my stomach from being tickled. I begged for mercy, and my cousins let me go. I was mad so I decided to play a little trick. I acted like I was really sick and started rolling around on the grass. Even the thought of grass stains didn't stop me. I had to get revenge.

I could feel my cousins' worry. I put on my best pale face. They were really worried. When they both leaned over to see if I was alright, I jumped up and started tickling them with all my might. They were soon begging for mercy.

We all went inside for a drink of water. Wai-po had some

duck claws waiting for us. At first, I thought they were disgusting, but after I tasted them, I found out they were delicious. The claws had very little meat on it, but my mom told me that the whole point was to find the meat and eat it.

Everybody, including the adults, took one. It was really hard getting to the meat parts. You had to twist it this and that way. Once, I broke the entire thing into a half and ate it. Soon, the duck claws were all gone, and the incessant chatter started again. As I stood aside, I noticed something. My mom's brothers and sisters' ages seemed so spaced apart. Her older sister and her brother seemed so much older than my mom, Aunt Guo Su and Aunt Guo Fang. Why?

My mom answered my question by telling me a story:

My uncle is 12 years older and my oldest aunt is 13 years older than my mom. My mom also has 2 younger sisters, both 4 or 5 years younger than she is, but what happened during those 12, 13 years?

Like every other girl in China, my grandmother was trained to be a housewife and started learning at the age of ten. By the time she was twelve, she was an expert on such matters. A long time ago in China, girls had to be married before the age of eighteen or they would be considered old maids for the rest of their lives.

Of course, my grandmother was married before her eighteenth birthday, and she saw her fiancée for the first time at her own wedding. Their parents had decided and arranged the wedding for them.

Since my great grandfather was rich, my grandmother had a large dowry. Two years passed and a wonderful baby came into the world. This baby grew up to be my aunt. A year after that, my uncle was born.

Three years afterwards, my grandfather left for Jiangxi Province to fight the Kuomintang. He was an underground spy, and held a very important job. Since my grandmother lived in Fujian Province, which is very far from Jiangxi Province, he couldn't communicate with my grandmother very well.

Meanwhile, my grandmother waited and waited. She heard from her husband about twice a year.

My grandfather was in a very dangerous position, and he had to be very careful not to let Kuomintang find him. By now, you have probably realized he was a Communist. He took crops from the rich and gave them to the poor. He did this by going to regional landlords and finding jobs. Then, he would rally the peasants to steal all the wheat, rice and grain. It may seem like an unfair thing to do, but the way the landlords treated the peasants was horrifying.

At the end of twelve long years, my grandfather finally came back. He had been shot in the arm, but at least he was back.

Another knock sounded. Three people came in. They turned out to be my cousins. They were all girls, and one was furiously combing her wet hair. Another was sitting on a chair, talking. The third was eagerly opening the gifts.

"Boy, have you eaten plastic or something over these years?" the girl that was combing her hair asked.

"Huh?"

"I mean, you're so tall. You must have eaten plastic," she told me.

Everybody started laughing. I didn't understand the joke but I smiled anyway. Then I discovered that she had said pig food, not plastic. In Chinese, plastic is *su liao* and pig food is *si liao*. Since my Chinese was horrible, I couldn't tell the two apart. When I found out what she really said, though, I became even more angry.

Was this supposed to be a family reunion? Well, I learned that day that family reunions weren't what I had hoped they would be. Nobody even paid attention to me but my mom, my aunts, Wai-po and my two younger cousins.

December 21, 1992

After an extended breakfast, we left the apartment. My dad told me that today was going to be a special, but somber day. He wouldn't say anything else.

The street was filled with noise. My grandmother was leading the procession. She soon stopped in front of a store. From the outside, it looked like a miscellaneous store. We went in. There were a lot of Buddhas on the counter, and the air was thick with the smell of incense.

Nai-nai picked up a bag of incense sticks, a bag of silver and gold paper, and a string of red tubes. I was mystified. What in the world were we going to do? Go to a temple and pray to Buddha? What were the paper and tubes for?

She paid for all the stuff, and we left the store. Soon, we were all on a bus heading for Fu Da. Fu Da stands for Fuzhou Da Xue or Fuzhou University. I tried my best to figure out what was going on. Praying at Fu Da? Did they have a Buddha there or something? For some reason, I couldn't imagine praying at a university.

On the bus, my mom quietly told me that we were going to a temple called Xichan Si or Xichan Temple. My grandfather's remains were there. The incense sticks, paper and tubes were for the visit.

I was silent from then on because I understood why everybody was so quiet. The bus stopped at Fu Da, and we got off.

At the entrance, my grandmother showed them a pass which allowed us to enter. Inside, they were remodeling the temple. Everything was in a state of change. I couldn't help feeling enraged by this desecration. It was as if they were converting the graveyard into an amusement park by putting decorations on the gravestones. A few foreigners were walking around, taking pictures and having a good time! Had they no respect for the dead?

A voice broke my chain of thoughts.

"They're changing this place into a park. They should at least give the dead people a quiet environment. They're not things to look at," my grandmother said bitterly.

I agreed with her. I was surprised that no one in America had ever come up with the idea. We walked past men tearing down old edifices and putting up new ones. It took all of my willpower to keep from yelling at them. I couldn't believe what was happening. The problem was that nobody could do anything about it. Almost all the temples in China were being turned into public parks.

Nai-nai led us into a little building. I walked past rows and rows of boxes and stopped at a ceramic box with my grandfather's picture on the side. A few flowers lay in front of it.

My dad reached out and took the box. The rest of us followed him back out. We bumped into a monk but he didn't say anything. We went outside, where my dad sat the things down.

"Yan Yan, your son, has come to see you," my grandmother said quietly.

Then, she started to cry.

"Daddy, why did they cremate grandfather?" I asked softly. "Didn't we have enough money to buy a coffin for him?"

"Yes, we did have enough money to buy a coffin. In fact, we had money to buy a lot more than one but it's already so crowded in China that they're not allowing any more coffin burials," he softly explained.

I noticed a lot of people were also kneeling on the ground with ceramic boxes in front of them, too. The crying sounded like the crying I had heard at The Vietnam Memorial Wall in Washington, D.C. Some were crying, some were silent, and some were praying.

There was a woman that stood out from them all. She was crying bitterly and screaming at the same time. Normally, I would have thought she was crazy, but at that time I understood how she felt because it was how I wanted to act. Obviously, her son had died.

"Ohh, my son, my son!" she cried. "Ohhhh, how could you leave me? Ohhhh! How could you? Didn't you think of your poor mother? Ohhhh, what am I going to do without you? Ohhhh! Ahhhh!"

The woman was letting out ear piercing screams, all incredibly sad.

My dad started a little fire, and we started throwing the paper in. The paper was supposed to represent money my grandfather could use in his afterlife. My grandmother lit the incense sticks and started a prayer. By then, tears were streaming down her cheeks. My parents' cheeks were also wet. Suddenly, I felt hot tears rolling down my cheeks.

My dad reached over and lit the tubes. We all jumped back when it started crackling and jumping around. It was sort of like a firecracker.

Suddenly, I felt a new presence join us. I turned around slowly. It was a woman whom I didn't know, but whom everybody else seemed to know. They acknowledged her presence without a word. It was Gu Nai-nai, or my grandfather's sister.

After a while of sitting and thinking, we left the place. We put the box back into its place and left the building. The woman was still wailing. The sound of it stayed in my ears for the remainder of the day.

December 22, 1992

When I was little, I would come to Nai-nai's house every Sunday. The two of us would go to a little street behind her apartment. There would be tons of people sitting on the ground with baskets of fish, crabs, shrimp and about every other type of seafood.

My grandmother and I would try to determine which basket had the freshest seafood. Most of the time, we just bought a few crabs because those were my favorite. Then, we would go home and cook them for lunch.

I missed those days so much but the crabs I was having were pretty good, too. The meal we sat down to on this day was delicious.

After lunch, my mom cleared the table while my grandmother washed up. I was starting to get bored. I had nothing to keep me busy. I decided to go call my aunt. I wanted to see Yang Se.

She answered on the first ring. I told her about my situation and she said she would pick us up. My mom had a bike so they could ride bikes and I could ride on the handlebars. The only problem was that she would be picking us up after work so I still had to figure out a pastime for the next three hours.

TV, writing in my journal and irritating my grandmother and mother were my choices. To my surprise, the afternoon passed quickly. Pretty soon, it was five o'clock. My aunt had promised to arrive a little after five-thirty.

I spent the next half hour downstairs window shopping. In the end, I bought a pack of Chinese gum. The wrapper had a cartoon on it but I had no idea who any of the cartoon characters were and I couldn't read a lot of the words. I'm sure it was funny but I couldn't find a reason to laugh. To my surprise and dismay, the gum tasted the same as any kind I could have bought in the United States.

At exactly five-thirty, my aunt pulled up on her bicycle. The three of us set out.

The streets were overflowing with cars, bicycles and rickshaws. My aunt told me that we were right in the middle of the evening rush hour. Everybody was trying to get home. We couldn't ride on the sidewalks because there were so many pedestrians. The bicycle zone was a lot wider than the ones in America, but it was still very crowded.

I was scared out of my wits. I couldn't believe that Aunt Guo Fang could go through that every single day. She seemed perfectly calm. She was also doing a good job of maneuvering the bike through the crowds. Even with me, she didn't seem the least bit perturbed.

Finally, we found our way out of the mess. I could tell by my mom's pale face that she had been frightened by the experience. My aunt looked at her and started smiling. "Aren't you used to it yet?" she asked. "Don't you remember what it was like, having to go through this every day?"

"Of course I remember!" my mom answered.

"Then, why do you look so shocked?" my aunt asked her.

"Because I don't remember it being that bad!"

My aunt just smiled and rode on. We were rode through a quieter neighborhood into another traffic jam. This time, we were faced with mostly buses, people, and bicycles. The bicyclists would get very close to us, scaring me out of my wits but nothing bad happened.

Before we entered her neighborhood, my aunt stopped and told me she would be right back. She hopped off the bike and went inside a little store. When she came back out, she was clutching a little bag. It contained duck that we were going to have for dinner.

We rode the rest of the way in silence. When we finally got there, Yang Se ran out and started screaming for joy. I calmed her down and we went inside. I immediately went into a room and lay down on the bed. I needed to calm my own nerves. I even checked my pulse to make sure I still had a heartbeat.

After dinner, everybody was extremely full. I stood up and stretched. I realized that I couldn't move very well. Yang Se was feeling the same way. She came over, and we plopped down on the sofa.

Soon, the remote control was in my hand, and the television was on. We enjoyed the first few minutes of it, but it didn't last. Soon, my aunt was yelling for us to do this and that. When we finally finished everything, we plopped back down again. We were interrupted again.

"Yang Se! Have you finished your homework?" my aunt yelled from the other room.

"I'll do it later," Yang Se answered nonchalantly.

"No, you won't. You're going to do it right now," Aunt Guo Fang yelled.

She appeared in the doorway. Before Yang Se could get a word out, her mom had hauled her into her own room. When I cautiously walked in, Yang Se was at the table doing her Chinese writing homework.

I personally had nothing to do, so I started flipping through her books. Her math books were simple, but the textbook work she had to memorize each day was hard. I probably wouldn't have been able to sit down and memorize all of it.

I sat there for a while, but I got really bored, so I went to the other room to look for my aunt and my mom. They were sitting on the sofa talking. I sat down with them and listened. They were talking about my aunt's husband.

She was in the middle of telling my mom what an ungrateful creep he was when Yang Se sneaked in. My aunt hurriedly changed the subject and made Yang Se go back to her own room to study.

When Yang Se had left, she started on another topic, "I don't know what to do with Yang Se anymore. She doesn't study when I tell her to and sometimes, she even talks back to me."

"She seems fine to me," my mom said.

"Oh, she's fine around other people but when nobody's here, she is uncontrollable. She used to be the smartest person in her class, but now she's at the bottom and always trying to play catch-up," my aunt complained.

"Yang Se is smart," my mom reassured her sister.

"Yes, she is smart, but she just doesn't study. Last year, in first grade, she always got high A's, and she was the president of her class. The president is the person that always gets the highest grades but this year, it's like everything just fell. Her dad left and she started getting horrible grades. I think it might be because her dad used to teach her at home, but now he hardly ever comes home," my aunt cried.

"Well, you could teach her," my mom suggested.

"But I don't know how. Her dad always had a lot of patience but my patience wears thin easily. I end up yelling to make her understand things. Usually when I teach her, she ends up crying, and I end up with a headache. And then, nobody learns anything," my aunt explained miserably. There was a long pause. Then finally she said, "I just don't know what to do with her," when she could no longer bear the silence.

"Mom! Can you come here?" Yang Se yelled from the other room.

My aunt got up and left the room. My mom and I followed to see what was the matter. Yang Se needed someone to quiz her over the next day's test. I found out that they had tests every single day.

I listened as Yang Se kept on making mistakes. Pretty soon, her mom started getting impatient. You could tell by the way she was clenching her teeth. My mom and I both knew she would blow up soon, but we couldn't do anything about it.

"God! Do you ever study for these tests? What's the use of me quizzing you if you don't know a single question?" her mom screamed.

I wanted to cover my ears. Yang Se stared at her mom with big eyes. Tears were brimming at the corner of her eyes.

We all knew the dam would soon burst. Then it did.

Yang Se's sobs filled the entire room. They paralleled her mom's yells in intensity. My mom tried to calm her sister down while I sat there looking at my toes. Suddenly, they seemed to become very beautiful and interesting.

My aunt slowly calmed herself down and left the room. My mom took her place and started quizzing Yang Se. She could hardly remember anything in her emotional state.

My aunt went out to the living room to calm down, so I joined her. Despite her yelling, I knew that my aunt was actually a very warm-hearted person. She was just extremely pressured by everything that was going on. In China, competition in the schools start around pre-school, and she just wanted Yang Se to compete to the best of her ability.

Before long, she had a great idea. She gave me a book. I looked at it and almost groaned out loud. She wasn't going to make me teach her English, was she?

To my horror, she was. She started reading the phrases in the book, but her pronunciation was horrible. Even with the book in front of me, I couldn't bring myself to believe that she was actually reading the same sentences.

She must have noticed my grimace because she smiled and asked, "My English is that bad, huh?"

I really wanted to lie but all I did was nod meekly and say, "But you'll improve after a little practice."

At that moment, Yang Se started yelling for her mom. My aunt went into the bedroom, and I followed. Sometimes Yang Se could be a lifesaver. She started whining to her mom about letting us stay overnight. After a brief discussion, we decided that staying was definitely the right choice.

Yang Se and I jumped onto the bed, and we started talking until our moms came in to remind us of the long day ahead.

December 23, 1992

I glanced at the clock. It was only six-thirty. I thought about complaining about getting up so early, but I quickly discarded that idea. It apparently wouldn't do much good. My aunt had a decisive look on her face that told me not to mess with her.

By the time I stumbled into the kitchen, breakfast was already on the table. We all sat down. I didn't eat much since I usually do not have breakfast. Then I had the pleasure of clearing the table.

While I was doing that, Yang Se left the apartment to get milk. That brought up an old memory.

When I was really small, we lived at the Institute of Research on the Structure of Matter, or Wugou Suo, a center where my dad worked. Every morning, at five o'clock, I would get up, get dressed, and go with my father to get the milk from the Wugou Suo's central office. When I was three, I only could get one bottle. When I was four, I got two. One day, I came home and I was grinning from ear to ear. I had managed to bring home three bottles. My mom was so proud.

Soon, Yang Se was back. Instead of bottles, she had two white, sealed plastic bags. What was this?

My aunt had a bowl of hot water ready. She put the two bags in the water and moved them around. Then she handed one to Yang Se, who was frantically putting on her shoes. She handed me the second bag and told me I could just drink straight from the bag. Then, she was gone. Since we were supposed to go to my dad's old workplace at 9 am, we were on our way back to the apartment.

After meeting my dad, we were in a taxi and on our way to Wugou Suo. When we pulled up at the gate of Wugou

Suo, it was eleven. The man at the gate immediately let us in. We went directly to the office of my dad's best friend, Mr. Si. My parents and Mr. Si eagerly started talking while he led us out of the building.

My mom and I were going to his house while my dad and Mr. Si were going to work.

Mrs. Si had prepared lunch before we had arrived, so all she had to do was stick the dishes in the microwave and then put them on the table. While she was doing that, her son came home. He went to Yi Zhong or Number One Middle School, which was the best middle school in Fuzhou. He was supposedly very smart, but I didn't find out anything else about him because he only spoke about two words during the entire meal.

After lunch, my mom took a nap on their couch. Mrs. Si and I talked for hours about everything. She asked me tons of questions about living in the United States, and I asked her about living in China. Soon, we were very well acquainted.

When I looked at the clock, I realized that more than three hours had passed. We were both getting a little tired, so she suggested that we go to sleep.

When I woke up, it was almost six o'clock. I looked around me. I was in the living room, but I heard voices from the other bedroom. I went inside, and I discovered my mom and Mrs. Si talking. They were going at it again.

Mrs. Si noticed me and told my mom about how long they had talked. My mom kept on saying that I was being a bother, but Mrs. Si insisted that I wasn't. When she saw that I was feeling a little out of place, she asked me if I wanted to watch TV.

I smiled and said yes. I went into the living room and clicked the remote control. I was watching the same program I had been watching with Yang Se the day before so I caught on right away.

I was so engrossed in the TV program that I didn't notice

it when my dad and Mr. Si came in. When I looked up, they were standing beside me. My dad told me we were going to Mr. Wu's house for dinner. Mr. Wu was another friend of my dad's.

We left the apartment and headed for Mr. Wu's apartment. He lived at another part of Wugou Suo. It didn't take long to get to Mr. Wu's apartment. He lived on the second floor, so we carried our weary bodies up the stairs. When we went in, I could smell the lobster broiling on the stove.

I exchanged glances with my mom. I could tell her stomach was also starting to rumble. We went into their apartment and seated ourselves. Their apartment was almost the same as Mr. Si's.

Mr. Wu had a wife and two sons. He and his wife were both in their late forties, and their sons were in their early twenties. His wife was a sweet woman with a face that seemed to always be wreathed in smiles. My mom and I were introduced to them.

After a while, I decided I needed some fresh air, so I went outside. A man came up the stairs. He turned out to be Mr. Song. When he saw me he exclaimed, "Hi, Gao Qian!" In China, people always say your last name first.

Another man came out of the next door apartment. He was smoking a cigarette and looking at me weirdly. Suddenly, a change came over him.

He started smiling and came over and asked, "You're Gao Qian?"

At first, I didn't know what to say. To my relief, at that moment, my mom walked out. A smile immediately spread over her face.

"Oh my God! Old Zheng!" my mom exclaimed. "What are you doing here?"

"Guo Xu!" he yelled with his loud, booming voice.

"When did you move over here?" my mom asked.

"A few months ago. Where have you been all these years?" he asked.

"America, where else?" my mom answered.

He shepherded us into his apartment and asked me, "How did you get so tall? Last time I saw you, you were shorter than my daughter!"

I noticed his daughter standing at the door. She looked like she was about five or six years old. He started questioning my mom about the United States. In his loud, resonant voice, he practically screamed "Do you remember me?"

I shook my head.

My mom intervened, "Remember? He was our neighbor."

I shook my head again. My mom answered a few of his questions, but she was eager to get back to Mr. Wu's house because she was afraid dinner would be starting. She explained that we had to get back to our dinner party, and he reluctantly said goodbye as we excused ourselves.

Everyone was ready for dinner but Mr. Wu's wife was still in the kitchen cooking. My mom was a little embarrassed by this, so she went to check on her. The two women returned to the table together. My mom urged her to sit down, and soon we began to eat ravenously.

The talk was flying around like bits of paper floating around in the wind. I listened to about five different conversations around the table.

After a magnificent dinner, everyone assembled outside on the porch. When I came out, Mrs. Wu immediately raced over and pulled me back into the apartment. I was a little surprised, but I knew she probably just wanted to give me something or other.

She disappeared into the kitchen while I stood in the dark hallway. I heard rustling noises and two voices, then she came scrambling out of the kitchen. There was a heavy bag in her hand.

Mrs. Wu handed the bag to me and said, "Hope you enjoy this. I bought them yesterday."

I peeked in. Inside, there was an assortment of everything. Most were edible. There were fruits I couldn't identify, different types of candy, chocolate and about everything else on this side of the earth. There was even a bag of sunflower seeds.

At first, I was a little doubtful about taking everything, but when I expressed my doubts Mrs. Wu cut in and assured me that it wasn't much. I decided I would let my mom fight over it with her.

We walked back out the door. My mom looked at me and gave me a questioning look. I handed her the bag of goodies. She took it and looked in, and soon, the two women were fighting over whether or not I should take it.

In the end, Mrs. Wu won the argument. My mom took the bag of goodies and looked dejected. I know people do that to be polite, but sometimes I think my mom actually enjoys fighting over things like that.

At the end of the evening, our goodbyes were short. We all walked down the sidewalk together. Our little group included Mr. Si, Mr. Song and his wife, and our family. Soon, we were at the hill, where we took our leave.

Soon, we were on the dirt road. It was pitch dark. If it had not been for the occasional stores at the side of the road, we wouldn't have been able to see a single thing. We walked for a long time. Finally, we came to a huge street and spotted a few taxis. My dad waved one over, and we got in and headed for home.

December 24, 1992

The morning rain woke me up. I had almost forgotten what rain sounded like on a roof. In all the hotels, we never got a chance to stay on the very top floor where you could hear the pitter-patter of the rain.

I sat up in the bed. After a while, the noise began to play a rhythm in my head. There was no way I could fall asleep again.

I went into the kitchen. My grandmother was in there. She was bustling around, looking at this and that and cleaning up this and that. When she saw me, she was really surprised. "So, lazybones pulled herself out of bed today?" my grandmother asked.

"Yes and I'm not tired either."

"Then, you can help me with breakfast," she instructed.

"Nai-nai, for some reason, I suddenly feel tired," I claimed. I faked a yawn. "I think I might just go back to bed."

"Oh no, you don't."

Soon, I was busy helping her in the kitchen. I tried to tell her I was catching a cold, but she didn't buy it. She wouldn't budge a bit even when I threatened that I might die from a disease.

I worked for a while, but then I had the perfect excuse. I told her I had to go use the restroom. In a matter of seconds, I was gone. I didn't care if she thought I had bladder problems. I wouldn't be back for a while.

The other bedroom upstairs seemed like a good hiding place. She wouldn't go look for me, would she? I didn't think so. I was climbing up the stairs when I heard the door of the bedroom open. I groaned.

It was my mom. She made me accompany her back into the kitchen. When we got there, I was so relieved. My grandmother was no longer there. I figured I would have to fall asleep before she came back. I jumped onto the bed and feigned sleepiness. I even fooled myself. Soon, I was really snoring.

The clock read ten when I peeked through my eyelids. Nobody was around. I jumped out of bed and looked around. They were gone. The window was open so I stuck my head out. The sun seemed to be having a fight with the clouds.

I found my mom in her room, gathering up the presents she had brought with us from America.

"Where are you going?" I asked.

"Liu Xiaoru's house."

"Oh." Mrs. Liu was one of my parents' friends. She had been my dad's English teacher in China a long time ago. My dad and Mr. Si had attended her class and later, they became good friends.

"You're going to stay home," my mom suddenly told me.

"Why? I want to go, too," I complained.

"We won't be long," my mom insisted. "You can call your aunt."

"Okay," I agreed, after some thought.

I called my aunt and arranged for her to come by at four. Then, I decided to take a walk outside.

The sun had won the fight with the cloud. It was shining like it was afraid it would never be allowed the chance again. I didn't know Fuzhou very well yet. I just wanted to get out of the apartment, but I couldn't go by myself so my grandmother had to take me.

To my surprise, my grandmother was eager to take a walk. She told me about a place where we could go shopping. According to her, it was called Business City.

I understood why Business was in the name but I didn't understand City. Was it put there to make the name sound good? When I got there, though, it really was like a little city where I could shop. It might as well have been a miniature city with no inhabitants, just shoppers.

I wanted to jump for joy. We were about to play my favorite sport. My grandmother just smiled when I told her this. She said that too much shopping was bad for me.

Before she could say anymore, I started running. She had no choice but to follow me. We were soon in a store.

I couldn't believe my eyes. Since I was expecting a tiny mall, it was a complete surprise to see the huge creation. I saw funny posters of elves and Santa Clauses. It was almost as if I had gone back to the United States.

I started walking around. There were three floors and two sections of the mall. The stores varied in size and shape and in what they sold.

Some stores had pieces of cardboard for walls. Some had things they had propped up, but none had a real wall. They didn't have doors either. We just walked straight in.

The first store was for teenagers. They sold everything from tennis shoes to dresses.

After that, we walked past a lot more before I found another one I liked. It was a small jewelry store, which mostly sold earrings. I went in because the earrings had attracted me and also because my grandmother had told me her godson owned the store. She had wanted to see if he was there so that she could introduce me, but we didn't find him.

The rest of the afternoon passed in a blur. All I know is that I bought so much stuff that my grandmother almost had a heart attack. She was very shocked so she started telling me a story about children that shouldn't buy anything at all. I felt guilty but I couldn't do anything about it. I am a shop-a-holic.

December 25, 1992

Suddenly, I rocketed out of bed. What was I doing in bed on Christmas? I hurriedly got my presents out from under the bed where I had hidden them. When my parents saw that I was awake, they went and got their presents.

I got two hundred yuan from my parents and a skirt and blouse from Nai-nai. I gave my mom a blouse, and both my dad and my grandmother a glass figurine. We all had a wonderful Christmas morning.

After lunch, we discussed the plans for the day. According to my dad and Nai-nai, we were going to visit Nai-nai's uncle who would be my great great-uncle. I couldn't wait. I wonder if he would be as old as I imagined.

My parents said they wanted to take the bus, but my grandmother said she wanted to ride in a bicycle rickshaw. I decided to go with her. Anyway, the rickshaw would be more comfortable, and I would get some fresh air.

Nai-nai led us out of the apartment. My parents headed for the bus stop, and my grandmother started waving for a rickshaw. Soon, one stopped in front of us. We got on and told him our destination.

Soon, we were going down the street. The ride was all twists and turns. The roads weren't well paved so the ride was bumpy. My grandmother and I had to hold on to the side of the rickshaw to keep from falling out.

Finally, we arrived at the place. My grandmother and I were both pale-faced when we got off the rickshaw. My grandmother paid the man and he sped off.

My mom and dad arrived a few minutes later, and we were soon knocking on a door. An elderly man opened the door, and my dad immediately recognized him as his great-uncle. He welcomed us with his hoarse voice. Then, we were greeted by another man who turned out to be my great-uncle. He was about as old as my dad, yet he was in a whole different generation.

I figured all this out while I was studying their faces. They were talking about things I had no understanding of, such as illnesses. The first thing I noticed was that my great-uncle looked a lot younger than my grandmother and that he enjoyed talking about illnesses. I also found out that he had a daughter who was only about two or three years older than me. If we were calling each other by the appropriate names, I would have to call her Aunt Tao-hong.

My great great-uncle looked at the bags my dad was carrying. Like other polite Chinese people, he didn't open the bags when they were presented to him. He put them on the table politely. I think he did this very expertly because I know if I was the one receiving the gift, my face would tell everybody that I wanted them to leave so I could open my presents.

"Where's aunty?" my grandmother asked.

"Oh, she's feeling sick these days. She's in bed with some illness," her uncle answered.

"That's terrible."

Suddenly, my great great-uncle didn't seem to want to dwell on unhappy subjects so he changed it to our life in America. For some reason, I knew he was going to do that. My dad answered his questions willingly. My mom and I did the same.

"So, what do you do every day?" he asked, aiming a question at me.

I told him about school and about all my classes. Then I told him about what I did at home the rest of the time. Then, I told him about the instruments I played: piano and violin. He just chuckled at that. What was so funny about playing a piano or violin?

After asking me these questions, he kind of shoved me aside like a fly and started talking to my parents and Nai-nai as if I wasn't there. I wasn't used to this yet, but I knew it would be happening a lot with older people, so I decided I would just try and get used to it.

I wish the children were as important to the Chinese as

the Americans. Unfortunately, I had to grow about another fifty to sixty years before I could be considered a well-respected elder in China. It would be best if I was twelve in the United States and seventy in China.

After a brief visit, we left. The minute we stepped away from the apartment I felt very much relieved. Fresh air cleared my mind and I could suddenly think again. The apartment had been so stuffy and dark that I felt like I was being put in a coffin while I was alive and well.

My grandmother said that the place we would be going to next was my Gu Nai-nai's apartment. I remembered her from last time. I couldn't wait to see her again.

Gu Nai-nai accepted our presents pretty much the same way as my great great-uncle. She put them aside and started talking.

The thing I noticed when I walked in was that Gu Nai-nai had cut her hair. I mentioned it to her, but she said her hair had looked that way for a long time. I wasn't sure but there seemed to be a difference. I decided to ask her some more questions.

"Remember when we went to that restaurant? You had longer hair then," I told her.

When I said this, my grandmother laughed. "This is not the same Gu Nai-nai."

"Huh?"

"They're twins," my grandmother explained.

I didn't believe her. Twins? My grandmother must have been kidding, I thought. Gu Nai-nai nodded and she smiled at me. Gradually, I started to spot differences.

First of all, this Gu Nai-nai was much quieter than the other. The other had also seemed a little funnier and more outgoing than this one. There were many more differences I probably noticed right away subconsciously but had not really paid much attention to.

She and her husband kept on asking us questions about our life in America. They asked me about school. They asked my dad about his job and they asked my mom about the culture shock.

The whole time we were talking, talking and talking. I felt more comfortable talking around Gu Nai-nai because she seemed to expect me to talk and not be quiet.

We had almost been there for an hour when my grandmother started making excuses about leaving. She seemed to be good at doing things like that because she had done the same thing at her uncle's house.

On the way back to Gu Nai-nai's house, I spotted a door that had seemed suspicious to me. There was a poster on the door, so I walked closer. Although I cannot read Chinese well, I had an idea of what it said. It was downright disgusting. Soon, the others came over to see what I was looking at.

There was an American model centered on the poster. She had shoulder length blond hair. She had on a black shirt, and she was pulling it up. The letters in bold type beside her said: **Three hundred and sixty-five days, every minute, every second, waiting for you.**

It was obvious what the poster was implying. I couldn't feel anything except disgust for it. Did people actually go in places like those?

My parents thought the whole situation was weird because they had no idea a city like Fuzhou would have something like this. My grandmother, however, wasn't amused by the poster. She was just as disgusted as I was.

We hurried on down the street and jumped on a bus.

We arrived at the apartment, and we had just sat down when my Yi Gong came rushing in. He was Yi Nai-nai's (my grandmother's sister) husband, and had just gotten into town. When he spotted my dad, the two of them started talking as though they had not seen each other for a long time. It was actually a bit touching since they seemed more like brothers than uncle-in-law and nephew-in-law.

Nai-nai started on dinner, and I started writing in my diary. My dad and Yi Gong were quietly buzzing away, and my mom was lying down... what a Christmas!

December 26, 1992

This trip was getting better and better for me. I made a deal with Nai-nai to take me to another shopping mall in exchange for letting her knit for an hour. What a deal!

When we left for the mall in a rickshaw, Nai-nai explained that she was taking me to a different one before we went to Shang Ye Cheng (The Business City). Was I going to complain? Xian Si Mall was supposed to be right next to Shang Ye Cheng. I didn't really care what mall we were going to because I was happy as long as we were going shopping.

We leaned back and looked outside. All the sights were starting to seem familiar now. The crowds of people, the traffic jams, the cars and buses and everything else was starting to seem like home now.

I wasn't surprised or disgusted by the bits and pieces of paper on the ground. I wasn't surprised or disgusted by the hundred or so bicycles on every street. I wasn't surprised or disgusted by all the little carts being pushed around.

All these things are a part of China and all they make China so much more interesting, surprising, different and more. They are like pieces of a jigsaw puzzle. All these pieces put together make up the country called China.

All these pieces make China unique. Tourists from other countries might come here and say, "Oh, how disgusting!" But people only say this because they are not used to the way things are in China. China is my home but even I felt that way at first. Since I had been in the United States for six years, I was used to the way things are in the United States. Things in China initially made me feel awkward.

If I was born in another country and I came to China when I was only five, I would have felt out of place at first. Slowly, I am sure I would have started to understand the country's uniqueness just as I was here and now.

It didn't take me long to get to work on this new mall. Soon, the clerk had brought out every set in the store. I chose six sets of jewelry: one for each of my teachers. I spent every penny of my Christmas money and some of my grandmother's.

My grandmother pushed me out of the store before I could buy anything else. The clerk, however, was standing there, smiling at me. I could hear her unspoken words, "buy more, buy more, buy more..." I was tempted, but we were already on our way out the door.

Outside, the sun was out. It had stopped raining. After having been inside the mall for most of the day, it was nice to see blue sky overhead. My grandmother and I walked to the bus stop where we were just in time to jump on the bus.

When we got home, my mom was waiting for us upstairs. She wanted me to get dressed, so we could go to dinner. I put on one of the dresses I got in Shanghai and joined my parents at the door.

We went outside and hailed a taxi. When we got into the taxi, my dad told us about the place where we would be having dinner. To my surprise, he said he had gotten us a room to ourselves at Tianfu Hotel. At first, he said he was trying to get a table in the Karaoke room, but then he decided against it. None of us could sing, and none of us wanted to. Having a room to ourselves would be much more comfortable and quiet.

When we got to the Tianfu Hotel, we were half an hour late. We went straight to the floor where our room was. The Zhu family was waiting in the lobby in front of the elevators. Mr. Zhu had an attractive wife and a son. They all accepted our apologies.

We were promptly taken to our room. Our waiter arrived to take our orders for drinks. The adults had wine and Mr. Zhu's son and I had Coke. I asked the waiter if there were ice cubes for the drinks.

He looked at me as if I was crazy, and then shook his

head.

"The Cokes are cold. They've come right from the refrigerator," he stammered.

"Well of course they did, but I want some ice cubes anyway."

"Why?"

"I don't know. So I can chew on something when I'm bored, I guess. Don't you do that to your drinks?" I asked.

"No," he replied.

My dad quickly interrupted. He explained why I put ice cubes in my drinks. The waiter finally understood. However, he regarded me strangely as he left the room.

When he returned with a tray. I almost burst out laughing. There was a pitcher of ice on the tray! He put all the drinks on the tray, and then went around the room, pouring our drinks for us. He saved me for last. He poured my Coke into the glass, and then used a spoon to slowly drop one ice cube at a time in the drink. I wanted to laugh, but I managed to keep it in.

Meanwhile, a conversation was buzzing around the room. As usual, it evolved around our life in the United States. I drank my soup and listened to my dad's wonderful speech about his job in Texas.

By the time everyone had finished their soup, the waiter had come back with a few dishes. He introduced each as he put them down.

The first dish was frog legs. The second was a vegetable dish. The third was one he took special care with.

It was a very small dish. The "thing" on it was so small, I could have eaten it in one bite. He leaned over and whispered in my dad's ear. According to my dad, the waiter had said it was the state-protected endangered animal, the pangolin. I was horrified by this news.

"If this animal is endangered, then why are we eating it?" I asked.

The waiter ignored my questions, and he continued putting down plates. I think he had already decided I was a lunatic that he didn't have to pay attention to.

Soon, he was leaving the room. I had finished my Coke, so I asked him if he could refill my glass.

He looked at me and asked, "More ice, too?"

I nodded. He left the room and soon came back with his famous pitcher of ice. He poured the Coke into the glass and then dropped some ice cubes in the drink. Just to see if he would get mad, I asked him to put in some more ice.

Unfortunately, my dad interrupted and said, "Qian, you're not eating ice cubes, you're drinking Coke."

The waiter seemed to enjoy listening to my dad. He quickly left the room with his pitcher. I couldn't hold my laughter in any more. I started laughing and laughing. My dad joined in. Everybody saw the humor in the situation so they started laughing, but when the waiter came in, my dad immediately put on his serious look and continued eating. The frog legs were unusually sweet. Our seafood was mouth-watering, and I enjoyed eating vegetables for the first time in my life. I saved the "thing" for last. I tore a little piece of it off and put it in my mouth. For a rare delicacy, it was the worst thing I had ever tasted in my whole life.

"What is school like in the United States? Is it hard?" Mrs. Zhu asked. "How many classes do you have in a day?"

"School is pretty easy. I have seven classes a day," I answered.

My dad cut in, "In the United States, they don't require as much as they do in China. She's in sixth grade now and her classes are a lot easier than they would be in China."

Mr. and Mrs. Zhu nodded and asked, "What classes do you have?"

"I have English, Science, Advanced Math, Social Studies, Physical Education, Gifted and Talented, and Orchestra."

"What is Social Studies?" Mr. Zhu asked.

"Oh, we just study things like history, present day societies, and things like that," I answered.

Mrs. Zhu wanted to know what Gifted and Talented was.

My dad answered that one. "It's the same as the 'quick class' in Chinese schools."

"Oh, and you have an orchestra?"

"Do you pick your own classes?"

The interrogation went on for a while.

The dishes were pretty much empty, so the waiter sauntered over and picked up the plates. Before long, he came back with another tray balanced on his shoulders. It was soup again!

In a matter of seconds, it was also gone. The waiter appeared again with more bowls of soup balanced on his shoulders.

"Wait a minute," I said. "Dad, is today the National Soup Festival in China or something?"

"Native Fuzhounese people love soup," my dad answered. "In Fuzhou, five out of ten dishes at a dinner party have to be soups. Sometimes, even the deserts are soups. It's just a custom."

This next soup was an herbal soup. It had a whole lot of herbs in it, and it was delicious! There was a faint smell of herbs but that only made it better.

After the waiter was gone with the plates, Mr. Zhu and my dad started discussing computers. Mr. Zhu seemed extremely interested in our computers. They talked and talked about them.

Meanwhile, my mom and Mrs. Zhu started a conversation, so Mr. Zhu's son and I were the only two left not talking. I wasn't about to start a conversation with Mr. Shy, and he didn't seem to want to start one with me.

I just totally ignored him and started listening to my mom and Mrs. Zhu. At least they were talking about things I understood. Shopping!

"Have you been to any malls in China?" Mrs. Zhu asked.

"No, but my daughter has," my mom answered.

"Oh, where have you been?" Mrs. Zhu asked.

"I've gone to Shang Ye Cheng two times and Xian Si Mall

once. My grandmother took me," I told her.

"Really? Did you buy anything?"

My mom laughed and answered, "Did she buy anything? Ha! She bought enough to last her an entire lifetime."

Mrs. Zhu laughed.

During this conversation, the waiter had started setting bowls again. It was dessert soup! I couldn't believe it! I was actually having soup for dessert. At least it was sweet, though.

There were little white bead things in the soup. They were really soft and they didn't have any flavor. The soup was water with a lot of sugar added to it, and it was black so I didn't know what might be at the bottom of the bowl. The soup was delicious, and I discovered that it was the perfect way to end a meal.

When we had paid the bill, we all took the elevator down to the first floor and exchanged goodbyes. Mr. Zhu and my dad decided that we would go to their house the next day.

December 27, 1992

"Qian, get up!" my grandmother yelled.

By now, I had learned it would do no good to argue with her. Since I had gone to sleep early the night before, I was feeling wonderful.

My mom darted into the room. She seemed to be unusually active for some reason. She told me to hurry and eat breakfast because we were going to Mr. Zhu's house.

"But I thought we were supposed to be there by ten-thirty," I said.

"Look at the clock," my mom commanded.

I glanced over at the clock. The colorful hands of the clock mesmerized me for a moment, but when I realized what time it was, I forgot completely about the hands of the clock. It was almost ten. Now I knew the real reason I wasn't tired when my grandmother called for me to get up.

When I finished breakfast, I raced downstairs to check on my dad who was – surprise, surprise – on the phone. He motioned for me to hurry up, so I ran back up to my bedroom and got dressed.

My dad came back in a frenzy. He kept on yelling for us to hurry up because we were going to ride our bikes over to Mr. Zhu's apartment.

I threw on a jacket, and we left the building. I had to ride on my dad's bicycle, and we were riding along just fine until we got to a bridge. We went under the bridge because that was the way all bicycles went. There were bikes going in every direction. Some were charging straight at us. It was so frightening and confusing that I almost fell off the bike. It was the biggest scare I had had so far. My dad hopped off the bike and started wheeling it through the crowds. My mom did the same.

After we passed the bridge, everything seemed to be easier. The roads were still filled with bicycles, but I felt like we were one of the crowd.

The road we were riding on was called Bayiqi Road. We headed for Liuyi Road. These were two of the biggest and most crowded roads in Fuzhou. My dad and I were riding along quite well when we remembered my mom. Where in the world was she? I turned around, expecting to see the excited face of my mom. Instead, I saw a stranger's.

I could already imagine the next day's headlines: "Overseas Chinese Suffocated in Horde of Bicycles!"

Ten minutes had passed, and finally my mom appeared. She was huffing and puffing. According to her, she had been delayed because she had stopped for a long time at the bridge. A woman in front of her had fallen from her bike, and she almost rode over the poor person. She stayed to help the woman back on her bike. Then she had continued to ride, but she kept on getting stuck in the middle of crowds. She had been planning to ride to Mr. Zhu's house alone.

We turned at Dongda Road and rode along. Then my dad turned again. This time, he turned onto Wuyi North Road. After a while, he realized he was lost, so we stopped to ask a couple of construction men where the building was.

They shook their heads.

"You know, it's a huge twenty story building," my dad explained.

"Excuse me, but do you know how many twenty story buildings there are in Fuzhou?" one of the construction workers asked.

My dad mumbled, "Twenty years ago, the tallest building was at Dongjie Kou. It was seven stories high. Everybody knew about it."

The man looked at my dad like he had been born on the other side of the universe. Then, they turned away.

After much pedaling, we found out we had taken a wrong turn and headed back. Soon, we were in front of Mr. Zhu's building. We were already an hour late. I do not blame them if they never wanted to do anything with us again. We had been late to two meetings in a row with them.

Mr. Zhu's son was waiting outside for us. I got really humiliated when I realized he had been waiting outside in the freezing cold temperature for more than half an hour. My dad was also embarrassed. At least I think he was. I do not know if his cheeks were red from embarrassment or from the cold.

We locked up our bikes and followed his son. He led us up some stairs. Soon, we were on a balcony. His son showed us the security system, and then pressed the button. We heard his dad's voice speaking. They talked for a second, and then there was a click. The click was the sound of the gate unlocking. His son tugged on the gate, and it opened.

We walked past it into a little hall. There were two apartments across from each other. His son knocked on the apartment door on the right, and Mr. Zhu opened the door. Soon, his face loomed in front of us.

Luckily, he had a good sense of humor, and he started teasing my dad.

"Yanding, hey, I'm a good friend. Why are you treating me so bad?" he asked.

"Sorry! I told you I'd be late," my dad answered.

"Yeah, but an hour?"

My dad laughed and shook off the other man's question. He then walked in. I had already gone in, and I was busy peeking at the apartment.

Mr. Zhu caught me, "Like my apartment?"

"Yeah!" I told him.

My dad asked, "How much did you get it for?"

"Free!"

"Free?"

My mom's eyes were ready to pop out.

"Well, my wife's department gave it to us."

"What?" my dad asked, not believing his words.

"My wife's salary is low, so they give things to us like the apartment," Mr. Zhu explained.

"Really, they never did that before," my dad pointed out.

"Nowadays, people are getting sharper. They understand the value of a dollar. If their salaries are low, which mostly are, they buy food items and other things from the stores. On the receipts, they write things like paper and things the departments really need. Then, they split it between the company and the employee," Mr. Zhu confided.

"But, then, wouldn't it be easier and money saving for the government to give higher salaries?" I asked.

"Yes, but the government doesn't know about this," he told us.

"Oh," my mom said.

She was awed into silence already, but I wasn't.

"So, you get all your remodeling and furniture from the department's money?" I couldn't resist asking.

I had been snooping around.

"No, we had to pay for that ourselves."

"How much?" my dad asked.

"We paid thirty thousand *yuan* to remodel our apartment."

My dad's eyes were also about to pop out. Five thousand dollars to remodel an apartment?

Soon, Mrs. Zhu entered and her friendly smile filled the room with warmth. The adults were soon bustling around to prepare lunch. I was just standing around with nothing to do. Mrs. Zhu noticed my boredom and commanded her son to let me play on his entertainment system. I wasn't too interested, but his mom would give us no mercy.

Soon we were seated in front of the TV. I thought I would probably see the regular Nintendo sign, or Sega Genesis, but he did not have such a thing. He had a little machine with Chinese words on it. If I read correctly, it said "Entertainment System."

I found myself looking carefully at the games. There were tons of pictures across the first one. It was the same with the second one. Some of the pictures had nothing to do with each other. I found myself wondering why they were there together. They could not be different levels of a game because even the players were different.

I finally found out that there were about twenty games on each cartridge. Some were really dumb, but a lot were good. He told me that in China, friends traded video games among themselves, so he had tried a whole lot of video games. Some of the games were repeated on different cartridges, but the good games were never repeated, so a lot of his friends bought a cartridge just for one game.

Soon, we were both so involved in a game, we did not hear his mom calling us to the table. She had to come back in the room to tell us to go wash our hands and eat. I washed my hands quickly, and then ran into the kitchen where everyone was assembled.

Mrs. Zhu made my dad, her son, and me sit down at the table first. She set out the appetizers and asked us to start eating. Her son and I were too embarrassed to start eating, but my dad acted as if it was something he did every day. He immediately picked up his chopsticks and started munching on an appetizer.

After a while, all the food was set on the table, and everybody was seated. This time, I knew I could start eating without feeling embarrassed. Mrs. Zhu started off the meal with an apology.

"Too bad our lunch won't be as elegant as your dinner last night."

"You can't say that because we didn't cook it," my mom replied cordially.

Mrs. Zhu just smiled and urged us to start eating. The food was delicious despite what she had said. When I complimented her, she had to say it was all my mom's doing.

Lunch lasted for a couple of hours, and then we had to leave. My dad said we should all go into the living room and take pictures. It seemed to me that taking pictures was my dad's number one priority in life.

My dad wouldn't let us go. He kept on snapping here and

there. I think he spent almost a whole roll of film at their apartment.

Finally, everybody started to get tired of it, and we went on strike. Mr. and Mrs. Zhu and their son accompanied us to the bicycle rack.

This afternoon I was going to the Children's Park with Nai-nai, but these plans were soon shattered. A light drizzle had accompanied us for most of the day, and in Fuzhou, a light drizzle could easily change into a raging thunderstorm. Needless to say, it did.

We had only ridden for a couple of minutes when it started pouring. All of us were drenched thoroughly within milliseconds. My mom absolutely insisted on going the rest of the way in a taxi, and my dad agreed.

We shook our soaking bodies and waved for a taxi. Soon, we were sitting on some towels the driver had so graciously let us borrow.

When we got home, we raced up the stairs. We washed up in the kitchen and then went back into the living room. My grandmother was already asleep so we decided to join her. We had had enough for one day.

December 28, 1992

My dad bought an apartment in the year prior to our return to China. Our plan for the day was to see this apartment and start a remodeling plan. My third Gu Nai-nai planned to accompany us. She was the one that had gone with us to the temple. When we invited her to come with us to see the apartment, she had been delighted.

After breakfast, we set out. My mom, Nai-nai and Gu Nai-nai planned to walk there while my dad and I were going there by bike. We were at the bicycle racks when I had a spectacular idea. It would go much faster if I rode a bike by myself instead of riding with my dad.

At first, everybody vetoed the idea because they said riding a bicycle in the United States was very different from riding a bicycle in China. In the United States, you didn't have to watch your every move on the bike like you did in China.

My dad trusted me and let me take a trial ride to see how I would do. When I first started, I was terrified. The street was very crowded since it was the center of business and activity. It was like trying to ride through a circus.

I started riding up the street. I rode slowly at first but the other riders were ringing their bells at me. I went a little faster. Soon, the wind was blowing through my hair and I was zipping through the crowd of bicycles. Pretty soon, I felt like I had been doing this every day.

As I started to slow down, I noticed another figure pulling up beside me. It was my dad! I jumped off the bike and wheeled it toward the sidewalk. He also stopped his bike. He told me that we could go on now because everybody approved of my riding skills. I yelled for happiness and then climbed back on my bike.

As I rode under the bridge which connected to central Fuzhou, I had one close call. A bicycle was coming straight at me and I couldn't get out of its way. The other rider didn't seem to have a single emotion flickering in his face. When he was a few millimeters away, I jumped off my bike.

I landed on my knees and the pain seared through my body but my fright and anger covered it up. A woman in a little store called out to me to make sure I was all right. She had seen the whole thing and she offered me her sympathies. I gave my thanks and then surprisedly looked around. I had not noticed the little stores under the bridge. They were extremely small but there seemed to be a lot of customers.

I waved goodbye to the woman and walked up to join my dad. He had not seen my accident so I had to tell him about it. My knees were just skinned a little bit but they hurt badly. I could still ride the bicycle but it was awkward.

Soon, we arrived at the apartment building. It looked like a smaller version of a huge hotel. It was ten stories high with white walls and red and white window frames. The windows were jade-colored and reflected the sunlight.

Our apartment was on the third floor, so we climbed up the stairs. My dad and I walked gingerly past the wood scrapings and tools on the ground. I could hear the grime slithering around under my shoes. For some reason, I kept on imagining that there were mice on the floor.

When we found our apartment, we tried to open the door but it was firmly locked. I tried the door opposite to ours but it was also closed. Defeated, my dad and I went downstairs to the second floor. A door was open, so we walked in.

Two men were busy painting the walls of the kitchen.

"Do you have the keys to all the doors?" my dad asked.

"Nope! We're not in charge of the keys. If you want keys, go ask the building manager. We're just painters," he answered.

"Do you know where the building manager is?" my dad persisted.

"She's probably having lunch right now," one of the painters replied.

"Well, can I take a look at this apartment? My apartment

is upstairs and I want to see it but I can't get in," my dad told the men.

"Sure, whatever."

We walked through the apartment. This apartment only had three rooms. There was a reasonable-sized kitchen and bathroom but the living room was tiny.

When my dad saw the living room, he couldn't keep from sighing. He had wanted a very big living room. I could tell this one was really disappointing to him. I comforted him and told him this apartment was probably very different from ours.

The painter saw our disappointment and suddenly, he had a great idea. He asked my dad to describe our apartment for him. He said he might have a key to a room like ours. My dad told him what ours was like. The men exchanged glances, seemingly waiting for something. I understood why when my dad pulled out two packs of duty-free cigarettes, they immediately brought out a key to an apartment that was right under ours.

We opened the right door and saw a large living room.

I heard my dad's sigh of relief. I didn't have to look to know that the living room was large but I did anyway.

We walked through all the rooms many times. I had to listen while my dad talked about which piece of furniture would go where. I kept on urging him to hurry because the others were probably waiting for us outside.

Finally, my dad assented and we left the apartment. The painters had left before us and had asked us to shut the door when we left.

When we finally met with the others, they were down there walking around with puzzled expressions. Nai-nai saw us first.

At everybody's insistence, my dad started telling them about the apartment. They wanted to know absolutely everything. He told about the bedrooms, the bathroom and the kitchen. Nai-nai had already been there so she didn't find anything new or unusual about it, but my mom and Gu Nai-nai did.

Their enthusiasm spurred my dad's own self-satisfaction. Soon, he was repeating his plans for remodeling. I had to listen to the whole thing all over again. We decided to stick together this time so I had to wheel the bicycle back home.

At the corner where the apartment was located, my dad decided we needed some pictures so he made me get on the bicycle and ride in front of the apartment building. He snapped so many pictures, they could have filled a whole scrapbook.

On the way home, we stopped for lunch at a wonderful little restaurant. We were planning to hold a dinner party inviting all our relatives and the restaurant had not been decided yet. At first, we thought about Tianfu Hotel but then my mom had mentioned the problem of money. It would take thousands and thousands of dollars for that to happen. Anyway some of their dishes weren't even as good as this restaurant.

My dad asked the waitress to call up the manager. They were soon engrossed in the details of the party. Although my dad had said it wasn't for sure, I knew he would say yes in the end. With the planning done, we went back to Nai-nai's apartment.

I told my grandmother that I wanted to go to the Children's Park, and she agreed to take me there the next morning.

After a short nap, my mom informed me that we would be visiting her old department and that I should get dressed. My dad had offered to sell them one of our computers. I was sick and tired of going to places all day long and I wanted to stay home. I tried to tell my mom that but she wouldn't listen.

I walked up the stairs dejectedly. I was starting to feel like a puppet. My parents held the strings and I had to go wherever they pulled me.

It took us about fifteen minutes by bus to get to her old department. We walked into a crumbling building. I couldn't believe my mom used to work in this apparently shabby computer company.

We climbed the stairs to the third floor where her ex-supervisor's office was. The whole building smelled of urine except for the supervisor's office which was filled with good, old-fashioned, fresh air.

When my mom's old supervisor saw us, he was so surprised he almost had a heart attack. When he regained his composure, he quickly asked us to be seated.

He kept on talking about my mom's good fortune, being able to live in the United States. I didn't like his way of talking, but who was I to say? My dad had really come to talk about computers so he soon got impatient.

It took him about twenty minutes to change the subject. My mom suggested that she and I go outside to find her old friends. I quickly agreed. We snooped around and finally found out from a secretary where her friends were.

Every one of them was surprised by my height so I was about the second most important subject in their conversations. My mom's life in the United States was number one.

Thirty minutes passed before my dad came back to join us. He was not able to sell the computer. With an apologetic tone, he absolutely insisted we go because he was expecting someone's phone call and it was supposed to be very important.

My mom seemed ready to cry as she said goodbyes to every one of her friends. She promised she would be back.

We took the bus home again and my dad went straight into the phone room, and my mom and I ran upstairs. Nai-nai was knitting again. I decided I wasn't going to be a puppet any longer. I was going to ignore everybody and go to sleep. I needed my rest.

December 29, 1992

"Get up! Don't you want to go to the Children's Park today?"

"No."

"Oh, you *don't*? Well, that's just fine for me..."

"Just kidding," I said, as I pulled myself out of bed.

I dragged myself over to the faucet and brushed my teeth. Then, I sat down to breakfast. My grandmother seemed to be in a good mood. She seemed happy to take me to the park. I hoped my attitude wouldn't affect her. I wasn't that keen on going anymore.

While I ate, I listened to my dad relate what had happened to him earlier that morning. "I went to Dongjie Kou to buy batteries. There was a man there and he sold me some. They were branded Panasonics. I asked him to let me try them in my camera flash because I had already been tricked twice by people selling fake ones. I tried them but they were no good, so I tried all of his batteries. I took out the used batteries I had gotten in the United States and tried them and they worked very well. Then a passerby stopped and yelled, 'Are you trying to prove everything American is good? What are you, Chinese or American?'"

A lot of people in China seemed to have a twisted kind of patriotism. To friends, they would express how wonderful America was and how much they wanted to go there. They touted that everything from the United States was perfect but if an overseas Chinese said America was better, they would ask with frightening disdain if you were Chinese or American. Even now I'm not sure what has brought about this kind of patriotism.

After a hurried breakfast, my grandmother and I headed for the Children's Park. As we rounded the corner and I came face to face with the park, I saw a huge make-believe castle. The entrance had a huge arc above it. It said Children's Park in both Chinese and English. At the front gate, we paid a fee. When we got in, the first thing I saw was a huge building. This one looked like a real castle.

There were huge aquariums beside the walkway. My cousins had spent hours trying to explain and I had not understood their excited chatter. Now, I finally understood what they were talking about. The aquariums were shaped like advertisement boards but they were a little wider. Each fish tank had a sign describing a specific fish and there were all *kinds* of them: goldfish, rainbow trout, catfish, lantern fish, hatchetfish, sea horse, toadfish and codfish.

In the center of the gigantic promenade were small fountains. Some were for appearance only, but many smaller fish made their homes there. A few of the smaller fish like the goldfish and minnows swam around in the freshwater.

Nai-nai and I went from one tank to another. Some of the fish were huge and ugly. Some were small and fragile. Some looked like the fish my grandmother brought home from the market and cooked for meals. Some were indescribable because all you could say about them was that they were weird.

I was leaning over a fountain, looking at the little minnows when I heard a scream from behind. It was a scream of horror. I was so startled I almost fell in the fountain.

I thought that if I turned around I would see an overflowing tank with all the fish streaming out. I started imagining the fish slithering in my shoes and socks. I turned around quickly.

To my relief, there were no overflowing tanks. There were no toadfish swimming around. There wasn't a single fish on the ground fighting or sputtering for dear life.

It turned out that a little girl of about three years old was scared of the fish and screamed.

That explained all, but I still felt a little weak. For some reason, I couldn't get myself to go close to the tanks again. When I told my grandmother this, she understood and we walked away from the tanks. I didn't feel much safer near the fountains, either. I imagined the goldfish jumping up and snipping at my nose.

Soon, the fish tanks were behind us and even more amazing sights appeared: ferris wheels, roller coasters and merry-go-rounds.

By the time I was done, I had ridden all the rides. The best things were the dragon roller coaster and the ferris wheel.

As we left the park, Nai-nai said she needed to buy something at the market because there was nothing left in the refrigerator.

The market was a mass of confusion. At first, I didn't want to go in because of the pungent odors. I could smell the stench of fish a mile away. In the end, my grandmother made me go in with her.

A few women greeted my grandmother warmly. People I had never seen before came up and tweaked my ear. My grandmother would say something about where I had come from.

My grandmother was persuaded into buying many things. Now I understood why she would bring home things we didn't need. Most of the time she had probably been pressured into it. I watched silently as many people took advantage of my grandmother's friendliness. However, I wasn't worried about her being tricked because she was as sharp about the prices as the seller.

When we finally left, I was carrying a bag full of pecans and a bag of clams. My grandmother was carrying a bag of oranges which she had been pressured into buying.

Someone called, "Jianmin!"

She stopped at the counter. An old woman with a wrinkly face had stopped us.

She asked my grandmother, "This is the granddaughter you were telling me about last week?"

I turned red on the spot, but my grandmother only nodded vigorously. The two women were about the same age and they got along especially well. When their excited chatter ended, I tugged at my grandmother's coat sleeve to urge her to leave. We were about to do just that when the woman stopped us again.

"Jianmin, have you seen my fish today? They're really fresh. I just got them," the woman pointed out.

Soon, we didn't have one but *two* trout for lunch. My grandmother told me she would cook one for lunch and save one for the next day. I just shrugged and let her have her own way. She was an adult and she could decide things for herself.

When we got home, my mom was waiting. She was reading a book so we tried not to bother her but before we could even get close to the kitchen, she was up and peeking in our bags. "Two trout, huh?" she asked, shooting a glance at my grandmother. She looked as if she were going to question Nai-nai, but, she happened to love trout so she did not continue.

The contents were soon spread around on the kitchen counter. Nai-nai shooed us out of the kitchen and started fixing lunch. My mom and I ran out of the kitchen and I told her about my morning.

After a while, I flipped on the TV and started watching a program. It was a documentary on Deng Xiaoping, the retired leader of China. It was incredibly interesting. I watched as many problems faced Deng and I watched as he solved them. All in all, the documentary seemed to want to leave the viewer with a positive image of Deng Xiaoping.

After the documentary, I flipped to another channel which happened to have a soap opera I had watched before. Soon, my mom and I were both deeply engrossed in it.

My dad came in at the exact time it was over, and as usual he was right on time. Nai-nai had just set the table. We crowded around the table and started fighting over rice bowls.

After the wonderful lunch, I went upstairs to take a nap. I was more tired by the day's events than I had originally thought.

After I woke up, I went downstairs. I saw that my grand-mother was playing mahjong with all three of my Gu Nai-nai's. When they saw me, they asked me to join them.

We talked and played mahjong all afternoon. Nai-nai brought out a few bags of sunflower seeds. Third Gu Nai-nai kept me at her side because she wanted to teach me the rules of mahjong. The only problem was that her Chinese was hard for me to understand. I understood a little bit of the game but I was completely baffled when she tried to explain how you were supposed to win.

All I really learned was how to set up a mahjong table and that mahjong was a gambling game older people liked to play.

It had been two hours and I was sure they were going to quit soon, but they never did. They kept going on and on. Finally, I asked them why they played so much. Did they not get tired of the game?

My grandmother answered with a sigh, "Qian, we're old and we know it. We can't do anything else so we play a few games of mahjong. It's the only game we have any patience and energy for. That's why older people play it."

I was beginning to feel bored of watching them play for so long. I was craving for a person my own age to play with, and I got my wish.

Yang Se came springing into the room. Following her were my two younger aunts, Zhang Jing and his dad. I was sur-prised. Why had they arrived so early? The dinner my dad had planned wasn't to start until that evening. I looked over at the clock on the wall. It gave me a start. It was later than I had thought.

More guests had arrived and I wanted to go meet them. The living room was much different when I peeked in this time. The room had been small even before the guests were there, and now it seemed crowded to the walls with all the guests.

There were all types of people: thin and fat, pretty and ugly, outgoing and softspoken, nice and mean. The majority of the crowd was elderly, or my mom's age, and then there were the children.

There were four more younger kids. One was about three years old but the others were our age. One little girl and her cousin stood up and stared at Yang Se and Zhang Jing. I could tell they wanted to play with each other so I gave them permission to go out in the hall to play.

As for me, I had a new friend. She was the other young person. She had shiny black hair that was cut very short. She had nice, clear features and she reminded me of someone I had met before.

Before we could introduce ourselves, my dad appeared out of the crowd. He quickly introduced the two of us and then told me that this was my aunt. She was my great uncle's daughter, Tao-hong.

The girl quickly intervened and said I could call her by her name. The girl had a soft tinkling voice with a happy and mesmerizing quality. It sounded like raindrops falling on a roof.

Suddenly, a man appeared out of the crowd the way my dad had. Who was this? I remembered his face but I couldn't remember who he was. My dad reintroduced him to me as my great-uncle, Tao-hong's dad.

By this time, I stopped trying to keep track of titles. I just started calling people by their names. It was much easier.

Tao-hong and I started walking into the hallway but we didn't make it. People kept on stopping us to ask us questions, and Wai-po also had something else to give me.

She stopped us and presented me with a solid gold ring. It was one of the prettiest pieces of jewelry I had ever seen, but I felt like I couldn't take it. In the end, after a "discussion" between Wai-po, my mom and my dad, I took the ring.

Then, my dad stopped me again and introduced me to a three-year-old boy. To my absolute horror, he was one of my uncles. I wanted to laugh. A three-year-old was my uncle? His mom – a young woman in her twenties – was my great-aunt.

When Tao-hong and I finally got out of the horde of people, I started laughing. I couldn't help it. My family was so weird. When I told her what I was laughing about, she also started. She told me that she couldn't figure out what she was supposed to call half of our family.

We talked more and more and I was starting to find out she didn't have some of the foolishness a lot of people had. She seemed to be a more down-to-earth person than me. I also couldn't get over the way everything she said had a logical sound to it. I wondered if they had a logic speaking class in her school.

Then, I remembered. Was she the person my dad was talking about that went to the First Middle School? Since it was the best school in Fuzhou, she had to have gotten a very high score on her achievement tests to get in. I decided to ask her right away if that was her school. I wasn't surprised when she said yes.

My dad called. He asked me to lead some of the people to the restaurant first so they could sit down and get a drink. The mahjong game was still going on so he had to stay. My mom had already left with the first round of guests.

Tao-hong and I led the way. We stepped past the tempting stores and restaurants. Finally, we reached the two story restaurant and I led everybody in.

Waiters and waitresses were scattering around. At the far end some were preparing the appetizers. Yang Se and Zhang Jing sat down on the other side of me although their parents were sitting elsewhere. The room was already filled with light chatter. A few of the older people had started drinking a little wine. Meanwhile, I was also having a conversation. Actually, I was doing most of the talking, telling the younger generation about my visit to Children's Park.

Then I went on talking with Tao-hong.

"What is it like in the United States? Is everybody horribly rich? Is it true money grows on trees there?" Tao-hong asked me.

"It's a little like China. We go to school in the morning and afternoon and then come home. Then, we do homework and other things. And no, not everybody is horribly rich," I told her.

Then, I asked her about the last question since I didn't quite understand it.

She laughed and told me it was a joke. Chinese people often said that money grew on trees in America because everybody from the United States seemed so wealthy.

Soon, everybody was seated and given a wine glass, even us children. A man I didn't know before stood up and made a short speech, which I didn't understand. It had something to do with good health.

I looked at Tao-hong but she had heard it. Everybody said cheers and we drank. I took a sip out of the wine but I immediately regretted it. It was the strongest drink I had ever tasted in my life.

One of my relatives came over and tapped me on the back. I didn't know who he was but since he was there, he had to be a relative. He started asking me if I knew him.

I replied, "Unfortunately, no."

He laughed, "You don't remember me? I was the person that used to come to your house all the time."

I shook my head again. My dad saved me by coming over and raising his wine glass. The other man finished his wine and motioned for me to do the same. I knew I had to get it over with, so I made Tao-hong drink with me. When we finished, our faces both had sour expressions painted on.

My dad laughed and offered to refill our glasses. Tao-hong and I both refused before he could get the sentence out of his mouth. When he finally left, we looked at each other and laughed.

Tao-hong's face was bright red. She reported that mine was just as red. I promised myself I wouldn't have another sip. I could already feel the wine going to my head.

It was a relief when the first set of dishes came out. The appetizers had already been there for a long time but I just had not noticed it. The first dish was shrimp, and soon, our table had devoured the whole plate. Many more dishes followed.

In a few hours, everyone was done eating but they weren't done talking and drinking. A few people who wanted to smoke smoked by the window.

After the meal, I taught Tao-hong some phrases she didn't know in English. They were mostly slang though I had no idea how she could use American slang in China, but she insisted I teach her some.

While we were talking, many people said cheers and drank but we ignored all of it. Soon, the others were pressuring us into drinking a little more. It would seem extremely rude to refuse, especially since one of the toasts had been made by an elderly man.

By the time we left the restaurant, we were both very red. My ears were burning up. I had never consumed so much alcohol in my life. I had two glasses and two small cups. I couldn't even walk a straight line. Tao-hong was the same way.

Back at the apartment, Tao-hong and I watched as the crowd started diminishing. Soon, it was time for her to leave. We separated sorrowfully and she promised she would come again.

After the guests left, the house seemed so dull. Half an hour later, my aunt was leaving. Suddenly, I had a brainstorm. Why did I not go with my aunt to her house to spend the night?

Since I knew my aunt would agree, I asked my mom first. She took a while to decide. After a long moment, she agreed and proposed the plan to her sister. My aunt immediately agreed and we left.

Aunt Guo Fang was a good bicycle rider so I wasn't scared

to ride with her. Anyway, I had already done it before.

We headed for Zhang Jing's house first because we had to pick up Yang Se. As we neared it, I noticed that many houses along the way were being torn down and that new houses were being built to replace them.

When we got there, my aunt parked the bike outside and we walked into the house. I got the surprise of my life when I walked in. There was no ceiling to the apartment. I wondered what happened when it rained.

I walked into the bedroom and found out. I started laughing when I saw an umbrella perched on top of some places.

Aunt Guo Su explained. "We have to live here until our apartment is finished."

I nodded and tried not to laugh. I walked into another room where Zhang Jing and Yang Se were doing homework. When Yang Se saw us, she jumped up and grabbed her backpack to leave.

They urged us to stay a little longer but my aunt was firm. We had to go, so Zhang Jing's dad took out his bike and Yang Se plopped down on it. I sat on Aunt Guo Fang's. Before I knew it, we were at Yang Se's house.

Zhang Jing's dad left immediately after he saw us in. He said it was too late already. We went in and I sat down on the couch with Yang Se. My aunt fixed us all something hot to drink.

Soon, everybody was feeling very drowsy. It didn't take long for us to change and fall onto the beds.

December 30, 1992

"Ahh!" I cried.

It was Yang Se. She had hit me on the back to wake me up. I gave her my meanest glare and started snarling at her.

"You wouldn't wake up so I had to hit you. Mommy told me to wake you up."

Yeah right, I thought. Suddenly, I realized she was fully dressed. Uh-oh. She might have been telling the truth. I looked over at the clock. It was six-thirty. I jumped out of bed.

My aunt was fussing with the bags of milk Yang Se had brought back. When she saw me, she threw me a bag.

Then, she and Yang Se rode off. I got dressed and drank the milk. In less than twenty minutes, my aunt was back to pick me up so I put on my new shoes and threw on a rain-coat.

The roads were slippery because of the storm the night before but my aunt was making good progress.

During the ride, my aunt's eyes were focused on the road while mine were taking in the sights all around me. We were in the middle of the traffic jam so I let my feet relax against the chains.

Before I knew it, my aunt started pedaling again. I tried to lift my feet, but my aunt turned and I had to hold onto her to keep from falling off. I was paying attention to hanging on but I had forgotten about my feet in the chains.

Suddenly, my whole body shook with pain.

It was radiating from my ankle. I let out a piercing scream and my aunt almost stopped dead in her bicycle tracks.

In a matter of seconds, she had jumped off the bicycle and was examining my shoe. Unfortunately, it was no longer a shoe. It was a few pieces of shredded leather dangling from my ankle. My sock was torn at the back of my foot.

I was expecting to see a bloody foot but nothing of the sort came to sight. The only thing that disgusted me was the enormous piece of wrinkled skin lying on my sock. It was disgusting because I couldn't believe that I was looking at my own skin.

My aunt saw no blood so she immediately assumed the leg wasn't in a life-and-death situation. She told me to hang on and we raced through the crowds. We finally got to a safe place to stop.

Meanwhile, I was biting my lip to keep from screaming. The pain was so intense I couldn't bear it. I felt a scream forming on the tip of my tongue.

It was a mess. Blood was smeared all over my sock so I took it off to see what my foot looked like. I couldn't believe my eyes when I saw my own foot.

I could tell my aunt was on the verge of having a heart attack, but she acted calm. She asked me to hang on and we pulled into the bicycle racks of her office building.

From there, I was carried piggyback up the stairs. On the third floor, my aunt collapsed. I decided to slide my way up the stairs. I tried to keep a smile on my face but it was incredibly hard. The pain in my foot felt like a hot iron.

We got to the fifth floor and my aunt's officemates gasped when they saw my foot. I could tell it was making my aunt feel even worse. A wave of pain spread over me again.

When she saw that I would be alright with her officemates, she ran out of the room to the building across the street where they sold medicine.

I had no idea what she was talking about but her officemates told me that my aunt was getting a liquid that Chinese people put over their cuts to make it heal faster. The word liquid alerted me to danger. I asked them, "Does it sting?"

"Yes."

I never knew that one word could cause so much suffering. I sat there, knowing I would never get out of the building alive. I can't stand things that sting.

She was back in less than five minutes. having probably run the whole way. The only problem was, I wasn't going to let her put the medicine on my foot. I protested for a while, but finally, I consented to treatment. Then she wrapped up my foot in gauze.

After wrapping up my foot, my aunt called my mom. She had an incredibly guilty look on her face.

Despite my mom's words of reassurance, I knew she was a bit worried because she arrived in ten minutes flat. She had ridden her bicycle. Since when did she ride the bicycle that fast?

I could tell I really hurt my aunt's feelings when I said I wanted to leave. But my foot really hurt and I didn't think I could keep up the false pretense anymore.

"Oh my God, I have enough trouble with my husband. Now, I have to deal with crippling an American," my aunt cried, as she wrung her hands.

I limped up the stairs to our apartment with my mom's help. I was hoping for concerned questions but none came. My grandmother just looked at me and started changing my bandage. I couldn't believe it. Was she not even going to ask me what happened?

My mom told her the story anyway and handed my grandmother the liquid medicine. My grandmother smiled when she heard about my aunt's unnecessary worries. She thought my aunt had overreacted. I agreed with her but I still wished my grandmother would overreact.

My dad came in a few minutes before lunch. At least he paid attention to my foot. However, he also felt sorry for my aunt. I couldn't figure that out. How could they feel sorry for my aunt when nothing happened to her?

The first thing I found out from him was that we weren't eating at home that day. We were going to a hotel near Wugou Suo. My dad had invited all of his friends. My dad said we were going to eat at the Fenghuang Wine House.

"Why are we going to a wine house? I hate wine! Anyway, what does Fenghuang mean?" I asked.

"Fenghuang means phoenix and Wine House in Chinese can mean hotel," my dad answered.

"Whatever."

"Do you remember Yanjing Hotel in Beijing?" my dad asked.

I nodded.

"Well, if you translate it word for word into English, it's really Yanjing Rice Shop or Yanjing Restaurant, yet it was really a hotel," he said.

I was confused but I nodded anyway. It did make sense, in a weird way. I had my best confused expression on but my dad ignored it. He knew I was doing it on purpose. I was told to go to the Fenghuang Wine House with my aunt.

On the way to the restaurant, we encountered some obstacles. The dirt road soon disappeared and we came to a wide and noisy street. As my dad had predicted, I noticed the hotel immediately. The only problem was we had to cross the street and we still had a way to go before we even got to the street.

There was no way we could walk on the street. There were way too many cars and other vehicles. Our only option was to go through the grass. There was also a problem with that.

It had rained so hard the grasses looked like the marshes. Water and mud oozed together to make it unmanagable. Somehow we made it to the hotel.

Restaurants were plentiful in the hotel so I was surprised we found ours so quickly. We were late because of my slow pace and crossing the "marshes." My mom had already arrived. The Wu family were assembled around our two tables and the other few guests were wandering around aimlessly.

We were the last people to arrive. My dad seemed to be in the middle of freaking out. When he saw us, he almost fainted. It was funny watching the faces he was making.

Dinner was relatively uneventful and soon, we were down

to our last dish. When it was taken away, I was so full I could have burst. I leaned back in my chair and stared at the food. Just doing that was making my stomach hurt.

After recovering from the meal, I got bored, so Lei, a newly acquired friend and I walked up the stairs and looked around. There was nothing interesting except a whole hall of hotel rooms. We walked all the way up to the top floor. There was a Karaoke room where people were singing. We stood outside and listened to people yell into the microphone.

Lei and I quickly decided it was time to go back downstairs. Everybody was getting ready to leave. It was getting late and everybody was tired after a long day. Our group split up and each went his own way.

December 31, 1992

I found out during breakfast that there were no plans for the day. Thankfully, my dad wasn't going to force me to go to Wugou Suo with him. That was where he was headed. I think he was afraid I would be too slow because of my foot.

My mom and I decided to go to the malls after lunch since we had some free time. She had never been to them yet since she left Fuzhou six years before Shang Ye Cheng and Xian Si Mall had been built.

Lunch was ready by one o'clock since we had a late breakfast. As usual, my grandmother had insisted on preparing it by herself, so all my mom and I had to do was to eat what she had cooked.

It was the perfect meal until my dad came bouncing in. He was obviously in a good mood. When he realized we had just started eating, he went into the kitchen and filled his rice bowl. He was done in the blink of an eye.

"I'm off to Old Song's house. I'll be back for dinner, though," he said as he rushed out the door once again. I was beginning to think he had a kind of food radar that alerted him to Nai-nai's cooking. My mom and grandmother just shook their heads when he left. Nai-nai told me that he had been a very excitable person ever since he was a kid.

After lunch, my mom and I left the apartment. We had tried to convince Nai-nai to come along but she declined. "You use money like you use toilet paper. I suffered enough last time."

My mom later told me that I had spent too much the last time we had gone shopping. It amounted to more than two months of her salary in that shopping spree.

After picking out nearly one of everything in the clothing store, we were ready to pay for it all. The saleslady's eyes actually glittered when she was ringing up the bill. She would be getting a sizeable commission on this sale. Her goodbye was the warmest we had received yet. It was a real one, but it didn't seem as real as a friend's.

Since it was four o'clock and my foot was starting to hurt and my arms were getting sore from carrying around the bags, we decided it was time to go.

My grandmother's eyes widened at the sight of the bags. I could tell she was trying not to ask but in the end, she couldn't control herself. She asked, "Did you spend a lot of money?"

"I guess you could say that," my mom replied uneasily.

Then, she showed Nai-nai the receipt. Nai-nai stared at me with her mouth agape. I shrugged. It wasn't my fault, I thought. My mom was just as guilty.

My dad finally came back later in the afternoon, he was wearing a grin on his face. He had a backpack slung casually over his shoulder and a few packages in his hands. They looked like presents.

I rushed over to get a good look. They were presents and my dad said they were for me. "They're from Kang Beiseng. Remember? Mr. Liu's wife?" my dad said.

"Really? Do you know what they are?" I asked, fumbling with the wrapping paper.

"No, she didn't tell me. They're late Christmas presents," he explained.

Everybody watched silently as I pulled the paper off the bigger present.

"Oh..." I gasped. It was a book. I thought it had the most captivating cover in the whole world. The title was *Down the Silk Road*. The pictures inside were entrancing.

The next present was a lot smaller and lighter. I opened it with more care. Inside, there lay five exquisite pairs of chopsticks. Each pair had a different design painted on top.

During dinner, my dad talked about his day. To me, his

day seemed like the most boring day in history. He seemed to think it was an interesting one, so I offered him my definition of "interesting" but he wasn't interested in it. Suddenly, he said something which made me shoot up and stare at him.

"What did you say?" I asked.

"We're going dancing tonight," he repeated.

"What?"

"Nai-nai's godson gave me tickets. The dancing hall is on the top floor of Xian Si Mall. You went there today, remember?" he asked, oblivious to my horror.

"Um, you seem to be forgetting something," I reminded him, pointing to my foot.

"Oh, that's no problem. You can just sit and watch," he answered matter of factly.

"Oh, thanks." I had never been on a dance floor in China before and I didn't want to start now. My parents weren't even that fond of dancing. There would only be one way out of all this. My dad wanted my grandmother to go but she kept on refusing.

He even said we wouldn't go if she didn't go. I knew he wasn't going to break through that tough shell of stubbornness on my grandmother and he always kept his word. If my grandmother kept on refusing, we wouldn't be going. I crossed my fingers and prayed my grandmother would be her stubborn self.

When she agreed, my jaw dropped. My grandmother never let anyone talk her into anything. How did my dad do that? She had not gone to the dinner party the night before, even though my mom had tried her hardest to convince her. She had not gone shopping with us and she had even refused to go to dinner that night at Tianfu Hotel. Old people are strange. Just when you think you know all about them, they change their minds!

It was almost nine o'clock when we walked into the mall entrance, which led us straight to the dance hall. Heavy metal echoed from the walls. I was surprised. Chinese people actually listened to this kind of music? After the song ended, another fast song started. I had been expecting to go into a little dance floor with very conservative music. I do not know how my expectations could be so far off from reality. The dance floor was huge. The lights had been dimmed and the music was loud and thrilling.

Before I knew it, I was on the dance floor.

After a few more fast songs, the slow songs started. New singers continually came onto the stage. My parents waltzed up to the dance floor. I sat down, feeling bored and tired.

My grandmother had been watching me dance before. Now, she was watching my parents with amusement. She seemed to be right at home in the room. With a grin, she told me my dad's dancing had improved. According to her, he used to be the worst dancer in the world.

"Now, at least he doesn't look like a complete klutz," my grandmother said with an amused expression on her face.

The song ended and my parents came back. The singer was a pretty young woman. She looked like she was in her late twenties. She was thanking everybody. I later found out why she was doing that.

During the songs, there was always a time when the music was playing by itself. Well, during this time, a man would come up and bring a huge flower basket saying, "Boss So-and-so bought this flower basket for you."

She would say, "Thank you, thank you, Boss So-and-so."

Then, another boss would get jealous and buy a bigger flower basket for the woman.

Then, the same man would come on stage and say, "Boss So-and-so bought this flower basket for you."

The woman would then smile her lovely smile and repeat her thanks again. At the end of the song, she would say thanks again. Then, the flower baskets would be returned to the dance floor. Then, Boss So-and-so would buy it again for another pretty young woman. I bet that was an easy way for the dance hall to earn money.

Three hours passed. They danced and danced until they

could dance no more. When I checked the time, I was shocked to find out it was one-thirty. It was way past time to leave. My dad looked very sleepy while my mother and my grand-mother looked like they were about to pass out.

January 1, 1993

"Your aunt Yeling is coming today," my mom announced.

"I thought she was Daddy's cousin."

"She is," my mom replied.

"Well, then she isn't my aunt," I reasoned.

"I don't care what you call her. Just be polite," my mom instructed.

"Okay," I agreed.

After a while, I asked, "What are we doing today?"

"We might go to Xihu Park in the afternoon and then we're going to Wai-po's apartment for dinner," my mom told me.

"Are you coming?" I asked Nai-nai.

"Everybody's coming. Even your aunt Yeling."

"Cool!"

There was another silence. I started thinking about everything possible when my grandmother said, "Your cousin is coming today," my grandmother repeated.

"Yang Se?" I asked.

"No. The little girl that came to our dinner party. There were two girls. She was the bigger one," my grandmother reminded me.

"But she's not really my cousin."

A few minutes later my "cousin" was at the door, standing between her parents. She was wearing a black sweater with balloons on it.

It took only a few minutes to get well acquainted, and soon we were running around up and down the halls together.

Somehow we got back onto the topic of Xihu, or West Lake Park. I had a great idea. Since we had nothing to do, why did we have to stay home and rot? We could always go to Xihu Park.

After much discussion, my dad said he would come along with us to be our chaperone. Our plan was settled. Everything was working along just fine. Then I thought of my real cousin, Yang Se. She had to come, too. I proposed this plan to my mom first and she immediately agreed.

I raced to the telephone with my cousin close at my heels. My aunt agreed to our plan and promised she would be over in half an hour.

I couldn't complain about the ride to Xihu Park. The roads took us through some beautiful scenery around. The blue sparkling lakes on our left seemed like diamonds shining in the sun. The little waves rippled through the cool water, making me want to jump in. The tall, imposing mountains on our right stood as protectors.

At one point, my dad pointed to a road. He told me that it led to Gu Shan or Drum Mountain, which was about the only piece of true nature in Fuzhou. I enjoyed the ride because I was pretty sure we wouldn't come this way again.

Abruptly, the taxi stopped and we were caught in a traffic jam. Nobody was moving, so the driver asked, "Do you want to get off here? We'll probably take an hour or more to get through this mess."

My dad agreed and handed the driver the money. We jumped out of the car and started walking. It turned out that we were only a few steps away from the park.

It was already past lunchtime. I expected my aunt would be getting impatient and Yang Se would probably be jumping up and down to see us.

When we got to the park, I only saw my aunt and her bike. "Where's Yang Se?" I asked cheerfully. Suddenly, I noticed something wasn't right. My aunt was acting very weird. She usually was pleased to see me. That day, she just stared blankly at me. I could see traces of tears on her cheeks. I knew something was wrong.

"She didn't come," my aunt told us.

"What happened?" my mom asked as she put an arm around my aunt.

"He took her," she replied.

She pronounced the word he with disgust. She explained what had happened. Apparently, her husband had come home after my phone call. He said he was going to take Yang Se to his mother's house for the day. She had said, "no," and they had gotten into a huge fight.

In the end, Yang Se was taken unwillingly to her Nai-nai's house. My aunt told us that she had told him to bring Yang Se to her Wai-po's house in the afternoon, but her ex-husband had not responded.

My dad quickly assured her that he would bring Yang Se. Her husband wasn't that brave yet. My aunt smiled but her eyes looked sad. She looked like she was about to cry. Finally, my cousin broke the tension.

She tapped Aunt Guo Fang on the shoulder and said, "Don't feel bad. I have an aunt who's divorced, too. She always fights with her ex-husband. Now, China's becoming the Country of Divorce."

Everybody started laughing at her comment. What she said wasn't especially funny. It was the way she had said it and the sigh that had accompanied it. Even my aunt started laughing. I could tell it was true laughter. Not some giggle she had forced out. The only thing I didn't know was whether she had been laughing about what my cousin had said or she was laughing because she was frustrated with her own situation.

My dad purchased some tickets and ushered us into the park. I could tell the adults wanted to talk without us kids around so my cousin and I raced ahead to it. We had decided to go to the amusement park first because it had the best activities in the whole park.

It took us two hours to go on all the rides. I cannot express how much better they were than the Children's Park. All the rides were really scary, especially the Octopus. It had eight legs and each leg had four little compartments we could sit in. We were spun around so much, I almost fell down when I got out of it.

My favorite ride was the Mini Mountain Car. When I first heard about it, I thought it was going to be the easiest ride in the world. When my cousin and I got out of the car, we were so frightened we trembled.

There were so many twists and turns. Whenever we turned, it was always at an angle so I felt like I was going to fall off. There were also mini free falls. They were mini but they felt just as bad as a real free fall.

When we got out, my cousin told me that this was a ride her mother had never let her take before. She admitted that her mom was right. She should not have ridden it. When I looked at her face, it was deathly pale.

My dad saw our faces and started teasing us. I decided to show him that I wasn't afraid. I grabbed him and walked toward the ride again. He started screaming so I didn't get to take him on the ride. My aunt was the only adult who had the guts to try it.

At first, I wasn't sure because she already looked sick enough to me. Anyway, she was having a bad day. I didn't think a scary ride would cheer her up. When we got off, I found out it did. Adults are as hard to figure out as old people.

Finally, when we were finished with all the rides, my dad said, "We're at a perfectly beautiful park, yet we haven't taken any pictures yet. Don't you think that's a shame? We have to take a few to remember it by."

A few? Yeah right, I thought as I stood up and smiled for my one hundredth picture. My feet were so tired they were about to collapse under me. I wanted to sit down desperately.

After enduring over one hundred and fifty photo opportunities, I swore I wouldn't take anymore ever again. My dad just shrugged. He had probably taken enough pictures of me to last a lifetime. When he was finally finished with his picture-taking, he left and it seemed that a weight had been lifted off our shoulders. We could finally walk around the park without having to stop and take a picture.

It took us half an hour to get through the whole park. By this time, every one of us was tired out. So we decided that we would leave the park and get something to eat before we went home.

We exited the park through the front gate, and there was a restaurant conveniently located in front of the park. We walked in the door and were greeted by a warm smile. My mom ordered noodles for all of us. Although the noodles were something my mom could have made easily, I was still eager to eat them. The day's activities had given me a large appetite.

During the snack, we discussed our plans. It was agreed that my aunt would take my cousin home because my mom wanted to go to a public bath house. She said she needed a bath badly since we didn't have one at home. The public bath house was for people who didn't have baths at home. I was surprised by this because I thought we were the only people who didn't have a bathtub or shower.

After the food disappeared, we went our separate ways. I watched as my cousin climbed onto my aunt's bicycle. Meanwhile, my mom flagged down a taxi. We were soon speeding along a road.

The ride took only a few minutes. Soon, I found myself looking at a massive and majestic building in a residential district. I couldn't bring myself to believe that this was a "bathhouse."

My mom and I walked quickly into the building. A woman sold us tickets and told us to go upstairs. We followed her directions and stopped on the second floor. At first glance, I could tell something was wrong because the man at the counter was staring at us.

Finally, my mom told him what we were here for. He laughed and explained that the women's baths and showers were on the third floor. We were on the men's floor. My mom's face turned bright pink and she hastily apologized. The man just waved her away.

A woman was behind the counter on the third floor. She

looked at our ticket and then motioned for us to go in. The first thing we saw was a room filled with people. Some had already taken showers and others were waiting for a bathtub to become vacant.

We were immediately let into two showers. We could have taken baths but we would have had to get in line. My mom said we didn't have the time since we were going to Wai-po's house as soon as we were done.

My mom was already dressed when I got out of the shower. When she saw me, she offered to comb my hair for me. I was really tired so I allowed her to. Before I knew it, she was laughing her head off. I looked at her hand. A broken comb lay in it. My mom had broken it trying to brush my hair. Was it that tangled? Anyway, she struggled with my hair for a while and in no time, we were out of the bath house and flagging down a taxi headed for my aunt's house.

"Yang Se!" I yelled as I walked in the door to my aunt's apartment. Yang Se came running up to me and started jumping around. My mom looked at her and laughed at her silliness. I was still thinking about her visit to her Nai-nai's house. I wanted to ask her a few questions but she wouldn't stand still.

A few seconds later, Zhang Jing appeared. This made her even more crazy. On the way to Wai-po's house, the two of them skipped around and did cartwheels while my mom and I walked behind them. We were soon at the apartment.

Wai-po opened the door and smiled her wide, toothless grin. Although her brown and rotting teeth weren't the most beautiful things on earth, I felt no disgust at all. After all, she was my grandmother.

"Is Aunt Guo Fang here yet?" I asked.

"Here I am," Aunt Guo Fang replied as she came out of the bedroom.

My mom looked at her questioningly. Soon, the two women were talking eighty miles per hour. I had nothing to do except to play with Yang Se and Zhang Jing. They wanted to play outside but I finally convinced them to come in to watch TV.

I got into a huge fight with Yang Se. She was driving me crazy so I called her a name. She immediately started screaming and yelling. My aunt and my mom came rushing into the room. My mom started scolding me because I was the oldest but Yang Se's mom seemed not to be able to control her anger.

Soon, Yang Se was a pitiful sight. Her mom was screaming and yelling at her. Zhang Jing stood aside and watched the whole situation without uttering a word. I think he just didn't want to be a part of this.

Sometime during this, Nai-nai and another woman walked in. As usual, my grandmother assumed I was making the trouble so she started scolding me. This made me madder than I was before.

Soon, everybody started to calm down so we finally noticed the woman standing next to Nai-nai. It was Aunt Yeling. She looked so different from before that I hardly recognized her.

Before she had come to Fuzhou, I had always told my grandmother I didn't like her. I had been holding a grudge toward her since I was three years old. When she was my babysitter, she had always been the meanest person on earth. Now, however, I wasn't sure how I felt. After all, I hardly knew her.

Ten minutes later, my dad appeared at the door. When they saw each other, the two cousins exchanged a hug. Yeling had always been my dad's favorite cousin because he knew her better than his other cousins. He also liked her brother Yeching, who was coming the next day on a train.

Dinner was soon on the table. I was seated between my mom and Aunt Yeling. Yang Se was trying to sit as far from me as possible. Zhang Jing was faithfully sitting beside her.

The platters of food had been set down in front of me. I wasn't about to think about where other people were sitting when I was starving. I practically swept the food into my mouth bite by bite. It was delicious!

Wai-po had bought the best seafood around. She told me she had spent the whole day preparing the meal. My mouth wasn't too busy chewing to tell her how much I was enjoying it. I think she could tell anyway by the way I was grabbing the food.

It didn't take long for everything to disappear. It was almost like a Thanksgiving dinner. The only difference was that we were eating seafood, not a turkey.

During dinner, Yang Se and I apologized, and we were the best of friends again. I do not know how we could change so fast but we did. I could tell my mom and her mom were really relieved.

My dad mentioned our dancing experience the night before, and Yang Se's mom mentioned how she loved to dance. We were soon planning which dance hall we would be going to that evening.

Since my aunt and my family had already been to Xian Si Mall, we decided to try a new place. Only five of us were interested in going: my parents, my aunt, Aunt Yeling and me. We told Nai-nai we would take her home first since she wasn't keen on going to another dance hall. She claimed that she had gotten a headache the other night from all that loud disco music.

The six of us set out of the apartment. Yang Se was left at Wai-po's apartment. She and Zhang Jing would be spending the night there. My aunt was also pleased with this arrangement because her husband couldn't come and take Yang Se.

Soon, we had stopped in front of our apartment to drop off Nai-nai. We all got out of the taxis and looked around. Suddenly, I got the feeling that I wasn't wanted. My dad was trying to get me to go upstairs with my grandmother. I stood up to my full height and screamed, "No!" He seemed to get the idea.

That night, we weren't let into a single dance hall. We

walked and took taxis here and there. Every club we went to seemed to close down just as we arrived.

After a number of unsuccessful attempts, the five of us were tired out of our minds and we had not even danced a single step. We were walking and soon saw a huge intersection. A food cart was set up at one corner of it.

My dad couldn't resist. The next thing I knew, he was sitting down at one of the tables. All this walking around had made me hungry again.

We ordered a lot of food. When I took my first bite into a stuffed dumpling, I thought I was eating peanut butter and sure enough, the inside was all peanut butter. I had never had Chinese peanut butter before.

Aunt Yeling and my dad seemed to have a lot to catch up on. Long after our plates were cleared away, they were still going at it. Finally, my tired mom suggested that we go to her sister's apartment to spend the night. It wasn't a bad idea at all. In fact, I kind of liked it: so much so that soon, I was sound asleep in Yang Se's bed.

January 2, 1993

Before I could leave the room in the morning somebody jumped out at me. It was Yang Se. "Aren't you supposed to be at Zhang Jing's house?" I asked.

She answered, "His dad brought me home a few minutes ago."

"Haven't you started school yet?" I asked as I walked toward the door.

She followed and shook her head.

"Nope, school starts tomorrow."

Breakfast was a quick affair. Mom insisted we had to go home the minute we finished. Uncle Yeching was coming, and Aunt Yeling was going back to her home in Lanping.

When we got back to Nai-nai's apartment, we came face to face with a band. They were standing in front of our apartment building. Each player had on a uniform with shiny brass buttons.

My mom told me that they were playing on the way to a funeral. I didn't understand why they played at funerals. I thought bands were supposed to be cheerful. I asked my mom, and she started explaining Fuzhou's funeral traditions.

In Fuzhou, the body is always cremated. Then, the bones and ashes are placed in an urn. My mom explained that it was a tradition to invite friends and relatives of the deceased to dinner. The band was used just to make things brighter. She told me that on the way to the temple, the band would be playing melancholy tunes but on the way back, they would be playing jolly ones.

We were barely inside the apartment when I heard a knock on the door. I opened it only to see a large man. He looked at me weirdly but he didn't say a word. A few seconds after that, I heard my mom's excited voice.

"Yeching!" she yelled.

Yeching? Then, I remembered. This man was my uncle. My face turned bright red and I was too embarrassed to even introduce myself.

My dad was more excited to see his cousin than anybody. They were great friends although they were years apart. Finally remembering us, my dad turned and suggested we go to lunch. My mom and I agreed readily.

I asked about Aunt Yeling and Nai-nai and he told me that they were off doing an errand which he had sent them on early in the morning. We left a note for them and went to the restaurant where my dad had thrown the party for our relatives.

As we were locking the door, I heard a song starting up. The band was going to play! I listened for a few seconds and was disappointed. The band was playing a slow, stiff and unmoving song. I told my parents my opinion of the band.

"Oh no!" my dad exclaimed. "They're supposed to be like this. They have to play sad songs on the way to the funeral. They'll be playing happy songs on the way back."

"Mom explained that already. Anyway, this is not a sad song," I told them. "Sad songs are supposed to move you. This song couldn't touch a pencil's heart if it had one."

We walked slowly toward the restaurant. My mom and I walked behind my dad and his cousin. They were still talking. I wonder what they were saying. They didn't have that much to catch up on, did they? After all, it was only seven years.

When we entered the restaurant, I felt like a celebrity. The manager came over and talked quietly to my dad. Then, he said something to the waitress. She nodded at us and smiled at us warmly. Then we were led to a table upstairs. What a life! I wished we could be treated like this all the time.

I had just made myself comfortable when two faces appeared at the top of the staircase. I stared at them. I couldn't see who they were because the hallway was dimmed. Nobody else had seen them because they were already too involved in doing other things.

Nai-nai and Aunt Yeling came out of the shadows. I was about to yell their names when my aunt put a finger to her mouth, signaling me to be quiet. I nodded and realized their plan. They were trying to surprise us. Unfortunately, their plan didn't work. My dad had seen me looking in the other direction and he had gotten suspicious. He looked over toward the wall and spotted the two women.

"Hey, I thought only children played those kinds of games," my dad called.

Aunt Yeling ran over and swatted him on his head. He laughed again to irritate her. For some reason, I suddenly felt like I was the adult and my dad, my uncle and my aunt were the children. It was time to order and once again I was definitely the child.

While we ate, the talking went on and on. Uncle Yeching was telling stories about his job. He was a police officer so he had great stories.

He told us that, among other privileges, if a police officer in uniform got on a bus, he was allowed to just get on and not pay. When I asked him if he took advantage of this, he said sometimes. I didn't think that was fair but he told me to think of it like a bonus.

He went on and on, talking in animated tones and gestures about different accidents he had witnessed and some dangerous situations he had been in.

Finally my dad stood up and stretched. It was his signal to everybody that he was finished. I had finished long ago and I was already tired. Soon after, Uncle Yeching stopped eating, and we were ready to go.

At that moment, I heard light strains of music carrying through the air. It got louder and louder. The song was full of vitality and brightness. I glanced out of the window. The band was coming! They were marching down the street and they were almost in front of the restaurant.

The others sat back down when I told them about the band. We had to wait a while because we didn't want to walk behind the band.

When we finally left the restaurant, the manager bid us goodbye and we stepped out into the street. We were home in no time, and soon thereafter, I closed my eyes and dozed off.

When I opened my eyes again, I saw a backpack out of the corner of my eye. Aunt Yeling was putting stuff in it.

"Are you leaving now, Aunt Yeling?" I asked.

"Yeah," she replied.

"But you just got here yesterday," I complained.

"My daughter's sick," she told me.

As Aunt Yeling packed, I started talking to her. I was in the middle of talking when she pulled out a little plastic bag. I looked over her shoulder and saw the most exquisite pairs of earring in the world.

I couldn't believe it when Aunt Yeling turned around and handed me the earrings. I couldn't accept them. They were wonderful and they probably cost a fortune. My mom also urged me not to take them.

However, Aunt Yeling was adamant. She said I had to have them. She wasn't kidding. At her insistence, I tried the earrings on. They were perfect!

I couldn't thank my aunt enough. I wanted to hit myself for forgetting to bring something. Of course my parents had given her a gift but I had not given her anything.

When we finally arrived at the train station to drop off Aunt Yeling, time was a little tight. We ran toward the entrance of the station. Any other time, I would have paused long enough to make comment on the litter all over the ground. We ran inside, and I hardly had time to think about the urine-smelling building.

We arrived just a few minutes before Aunt Yeling's train number was called. Since we weren't allowed to go to the train with her, we started waving as hard as we could as soon as she got out to the platform. I jumped up and down until she was out of sight. Then my shoulders sagged. I felt so beaten. I hated saying goodbye to anything or anyone.

It was dinner time. From the living room, I could smell the mouth-watering fish and crabs. I could already hear my stomach grumbling and rumbling inside of me.

As usual, Nai-nai's dinner was absolutely, heavenly delicious. However, my festive spirit was still a little dampened by Aunt Yeling's departure. During dinner though, my mother told a funny story that did wonders for my spirit.

Aunt Guo Su's husband, Uncle Zhi Xing and his brother had been working in a factory for more than fifteen years. Both brothers' houses were being rebuilt. Aunt Guo Su, Uncle Zhi Xing, his brother and his brother's wife were all tired of living under the stars with an umbrella to keep away the rain. So these four had gotten together and rushed to the director of the factory.

"We don't have a house to live in. We've worked here for more than fifteen years. Do you have a room or two in the factory for us?" asked Uncle Zhi Xing.

"Absolutely not! Why don't you go live with your mother-in-laws?" he asked.

Uncle Zhi Xing answered, "My mother-in-law's house is already too crowded. Some of her daughters are living there now since my brother's mother-in-law has died."

"Well, then go live in a temporary apartment," the director suggested.

"There are none available," they answered. "We have already been to your apartment building. We know that you have two sets of apartments. You have to rent a room to us, even if it's the bathroom. If you don't rent it to us, we're going to show up on your doorstep tonight."

The director was getting worried.

"Don't you have anywhere else to go?"

"No," they answered firmly.

In the end, they were assigned three rooms in the factory.

*Two of them were as big as classrooms and they were used
as bedrooms. There was also a little room cleared out for the
kitchen. They had succeeded.*

When my mom finished, there was a knock on the door.
It was Tao-hong but she wasn't in her usual happy mood.
Normally, we would have gone right to cooking up pranks
but that day, I was sulking about leaving and Tao-hong was
sulking with me. We were too sad to even think about being
happy.

At nine forty nine, Tao-hong's dad called, "Tao-hong, we
have to go home now!"
No, I thought but we walked obediently down the stairs.
Tao-hong's dad was already standing in the hallway when
we got to it. Tao-hong was looking at me with a forced smile.
I forced one of mine back and said goodbye.
Suddenly, I remembered. I didn't have her address yet. I
led Tao-hong back into the living room. It took me an extra
long time to find a pen and paper. When Tao-hong finished
jotting down her address, I took the pen and wrote mine. It
should have taken me a few seconds. Instead, it took me almost ten minutes.
As we were walking toward the door, my dad yelled, "Hey,
wait! Don't leave yet! I need a picture!"
This was the first time in my life I actually appreciated
my dad's picture taking. Tao-hong and I stood still while my
dad took five or six pictures. She didn't seem to enjoy taking
pictures but she was also glad it was prolonging her time
here.
We exchanged one last goodbye and then she left. I felt
extremely sad as I watched her pedal away. I felt like I was
being split into two parts. One part of me wanted to stay in
China with all my recently made friends and my relatives.
The other part wanted to go back to America where all my
old friends were.
The rest of the evening passed like a detached dream. I

answered like an automaton whenever anybody asked me a question. I never even really heard them.

When I got in bed, my mind was still confused. I thrashed and kicked my blankets as my thoughts took control. I never even realized when I slowly slipped into the wonderful world of sleep where nothing can hurt or help you. I had neither dreams nor nightmares.

January 3, 1993

Sunlight was shining through my eyes. It was morning already. After dressing in the other bedroom, I went downstairs to eat.

As I walked into the kitchen, my dad complained, "We don't have enough suitcases. We need one more."

I stood still. Suitcases? Oh my gosh! We were leaving Fuzhou! I had completely forgotten. A wave of sadness started to spread over me. I only had a few more hours left in Fuzhou.

"Well, go buy one then," I said.

"I don't have enough time. I still have to pack the other suitcases."

I was in a foul mood because I wanted to get a few more souvenirs. The problem was nobody would take me. In the end, Uncle Yeching relented, and said he would take me. Along the way we would pick up a suitcase.

We took the bus since we did not want to spend the money on a taxi. Since we were only going to Dong Jie Kou, the ride was not very long. In the end, I got a few souvenirs for myself and a few gifts for my friends along with the suitcase for my dad. When we were finished shopping, there was only an hour and a half before we had to leave.

When we got back home, I ran up the stairs and found my dad packing. Some relatives had also come, but nobody was talking. When I walked in everyone was relieved. They had been worried I would miss my plane.

My grandmother was frowning and making faces at my dad. I could tell she was mad, but I was not too sure about what. I found out later that she had yelled at my dad because she was afraid I might miss my flight to Hong Kong.

Mr. Zhu's truck came, and we put the suitcases in. Then we headed for the airport.

During the ride, I wanted to cry. I could not believe that I was about to leave all of my relatives. I could not believe I was about to leave my newfound friends. Everybody! Even my grandmother! How could I leave them? How could I leave her? It was impossible!

As I looked out the window, I remembered all the experiences I had in Fuzhou. I remembered all the people I had met. I remembered everything I had done with every one of them.

Nai-nai, Gu Nai-nai, Wai-po, Aunt Yeling, Yang Se, Uncle Yeching, my aunts, Tao-hong, my cousins, and many more faces flickered through my mind. I thought of everybody I had met. Their concern for me before had seemed so natural, but now I realized that nobody would act that way to me except the people who really and truly loved me.

As I thought on, one word kept on going through my mind. No, no, no, no... No! I could not leave! No! I wanted to scream and tell the whole world how I felt.

A terrible aching was going through every part of my body. Despite my complaints and sarcastic remarks during my visit, I loved Fuzhou very much. It was a place I could never dislike or hate no matter what happened. It would always be a home to me.

Our farewells were extremely depressing, and my grandmother kept crying. Actually, almost everyone was crying - especially me. I could not bear to leave Fuzhou. Even the thought of my friends in College Station did not make me want to change my mind. Of course, I still missed them, but I knew I would be able to see them very soon.

I was not so sure about being able to see my grandmother or any of my relatives again very soon. My grandmother could be a very stubborn person. She might not want to come live with us in the United States, or she might fall ill. I could not stand to think about that. The worst thing about it was that I had a feeling in the pit of my stomach that I would not see Fuzhou or any of my relatives for at least another few years.

We went into customs. I stood by the open door and waved

and waved until my dad motioned me over. With one last wave, I blew a kiss to my grandmother.

January 4, 1993

"Wof, wof!"

A wet tongue was licking my face.

"OK, Bobo. Down!" I yelled.

He kept licking me.

"Fine, I'll get up!" Sooner or later, I thought.

Bobo wasn't a stupid dog. It took only a few minutes for the noisy barking to begin again. This time, I jumped out of bed and flipped Bobo over. He had been sitting on my stomach so when I jumped up, he got the biggest surprise of his life.

As I was sitting on the bed, I suddenly realized something. This was the very last day of our trip. I was starting to tremble. I wanted to go home but I also wanted to stay.

As I slowly got out of bed, I silently vowed to spend the last day of my trip happily.

Helen was in the kitchen cooking. My dad was resting at the breakfast table, reading a newspaper. I sat down on the couch and watched him shuffle the papers around him. Meanwhile, Bobo sat on the floor, staring at me. Finally, his pitiful eyes got to me and I allowed him to sit on my lap.

Since it was eight-thirty, Sophia was long gone. After a quick breakfast we went to the North Point Market along the busy thoroughfare. Helen said that she wanted us to go there and buy some stuff to take to America.

There was activity all over the clustered streets. Now, however, the people around me were no longer a surprise or an annoyance. I felt like it was an everyday thing.

The only problem I still encountered regularly was with the restrooms in Hong Kong. And I had to go again. We found a restaurant and Helen handed me a bag of tissues. I stuck them in my pocket and started off hesitantly. When I got in there, I almost threw up. The stench was horrible. I wanted to die.

In front of me stood an empty stall. I kicked it open and locked the door with my fingertips. I looked around. There was the hole in the ground.

I looked down. The bathroom seemed to be just as bad as the one I had been in last time. I quickly used the restroom, and rushed out. I didn't even wait to wash my hands. I bet that would have been a lot more infectious than not washing them at all.

Helen and my dad listened and laughed when I told my disgusting story. They actually thought it was funny. I wonder what Helen would have done. After a while, we grew tired of shopping and took the crowded subway home. It was a lot more crowded because people were on their way home for lunch.

When we finally reached Helen's apartment, we were greeted by the very easily excited Bobo. He had started barking the minute he heard the key in the lock. When I walked in, I got the biggest lick in my life. It was Bobo's welcome.

After a long, relaxing nap, Helen and I convinced my dad that we had to go to the Pacific Palace. We decided to take a trolley car to this biggest of all the Hong Kong malls. My dad had wanted to do that because he said we might as well experience something worthwhile if we were going to go shopping again. He considered shopping in malls an useless activity.

The trolley car had two decks. The first deck was already crowded to every little corner so we decided to try the second deck. It was a lot better. Not so many people roamed about up there. We even got our own seats.

My dad suddenly had this great idea. He wanted a picture of this. Not again! He forced us to stand up and then he started taking pictures. I was really embarrassed because everybody started staring at us once the camera started clicking.

When it was time to get off the trolley car. I had been

taking pictures from all the different angles possible, and had not even noticed my surroundings until I got off the trolley.

I stared as my mouth formed in the shape of an "O."

Huge buildings towered over us. Sparkling windows shone in the sunlight. The young doormen stood in front of the buildings. Christmas trees and decorations were still scattered inside the stores.

Helen stopped in front of the biggest building of all.

"This is Pacific Place," she pointed out.

Even my dad was impressed.

Her voice had immediately told me I wouldn't be buying anything. I didn't really care. I just wanted to look.

Inside the mall, there wasn't a sound. I felt a chilly wind spread over me as Helen told us about the prices of this and that. It didn't take a minute to realize that most of the prices were in the thousands or more.

There were four or five floors to the mall and we went through every one of them. Every floor had stores, but there wasn't a single store that sold inexpensive things. After a while, I couldn't bear it. I was getting tired of looking at things I couldn't afford.

Finally, Helen noticed my frustration. She asked me if I wanted to eat something. I said yes.

Since we were right in front of the elevator, we took it down to the McDonald's. The elevator itself was also very elegant. It was transparent and cylindrical, so anybody could see who was riding.

When I thought about it, there shouldn't have been a McDonald's in Pacific Place. The mall was too fancy to have fast food restaurants.

To my disappointment, the line was very long. I guess people did like an opportunity to save a little money. When we finally got to the counter, I already knew what I would order.

"A cheeseburger and a strawberry sundae, please," I requested.

The store was so much like any other McDonald's in College Station that I had forgotten and accidentally spoken in English. Of course, the women didn't understand me. She stared at me.

Finally, Helen intervened, and she ordered for me in Cantonese.

I started off with my cheeseburger. I wasn't as hungry as I thought I was, though. In fact, I could hardly force down the food. Suddenly, I realized it wasn't because I wasn't hungry. It was because I wasn't used to American food anymore. When I realized this, I almost laughed. To think that I wasn't used to eating American food?

We sat there for a while longer but finally, I couldn't bear it. I stood up and looked at the other two. They followed my example and also stood up. Soon, we were working our way out of the mall.

Before we made it, though, my dad stopped. I knew what he was going to say.

"Pictures!" he yelled.

Helen groaned and I smiled. Even she was getting tired of his picture taking. We let him take a few shots, then we refused to take anymore.

Sophia was waiting for us when we got to the apartment. She was really happy to see us and she told me a little about her school day.

Pretty soon, Sophia was lugging out photo albums for us to look at. I saw pictures of her when she was a little toddler and I saw pictures of her in ballet class when she was only eight years old. I saw her school pictures and I saw pictures of her with her friends.

As I looked through these, I realized my dad was right. Pictures really were memories that could be kept forever. Pictures were things you could show others. Taking pictures is irritating but looking at them later more than makes up for the trouble.

By the time we had looked through all the albums, it was getting close to seven and we were starting to get hungry. Helen recommended one of those supermarkets again so we went along with her suggestion. Soon, we were on the elevator and heading out into the Hong Kong evening.

Helen led us into a huge supermarket. Delicious smells wafted from behind the little counters. Beneath each glass counter was a different type of food. We all got a bowl of noodles and my dad set off to get some other things. He soon came back with a bowl of clams, some bread and drinks for each of us. Dinner was good, but I was seriously preoccupied the entire time.

When we left the supermarket, I was hardly paying attention to anything. In my mind, five words kept on racing through my mind. I am really going back, I am really going back, I am really going back... I wasn't sure if I was happy or sad. I couldn't think.

I looked around me. Where were we going? We were walking away from the apartment buildings, not toward them. I didn't voice any of my thoughts because I didn't want to go straight back into the apartment. I wanted to walk around and make most of the hours I had left.

At that time, I only had one wish. It wasn't to get rich quick, or be the most famous person on earth. My wish was to visit every city we had been to all over again. I wished I could have spent five more days in China. One for Hong Kong, Guangzhou, Beijing, Shanghai and Fuzhou.

However hard I prayed though, I didn't get my wish. The best I could do was to make do with what I had around me and what I had in front of me. For some reason, that thought didn't give me much pleasure or relief. Thoughts raced through my mind but they went by so fast, I couldn't identify them. I felt like a prisoner trapped inside myself.

That night, I tossed and turned but no relief came. I kept telling myself that I would be going back to the United States to my home. It didn't work, I still felt miserable. As I finally fell asleep, I thought of the good times I had in China and the good times I had in the United States. There wasn't a better or worse. I decided that I treasured both my homes, China and the United States.

January 5, 1993 - Epilogue

It wasn't hard to get up on this dark and dreary day. I had been tossing and turning the whole night. I was tired physically and mentally. Fortunately, my physical tiredness was being pushed out by emotions.

The clock said five-thirty. Time didn't matter anymore. Nothing did except the fact that I was leaving. Of course, the thought of returning to the United States was enticing but my other emotions won the fight over excitement.

I felt like a robot that morning. I dressed without thinking, I ate without thinking and I talked without thinking. I did everything without thinking. I hardly noticed anything during the taxi ride. I hardly noticed the airport.

All I know is that I have this gnawing pain inside of me that I wish could be replaced by physical pain. At least physical pain goes away, but the mental anguish I am feeling will probably stay with me much longer. My foot is a good example. It bled and bled when I injured it riding with my aunt on her bicycle. Now, it is just a scar and seems so trivial.

My mental pain, on the other hand, is far from trivial. I know it will go away but it will always be somewhere in my mind.

When I first started out on this trip, I felt pain, excitement, fear and sorrow. I am leaving now and I am thinking of the exact same things. Some of my reasons are still the same, and some are completely different. Almost every one of them is like a dagger going straight into my heart.

Pain is leaving everyone in China. It is leaving my new friends and it is leaving places I love.

Excitement! It is the thought of returning to the U.S. It is the thought of my old friends. It is the thought of the life I left behind.

I no longer have a fear of being lost or abducted. Instead,

I have a fear of never returning. I fear never seeing my loved ones in China again. Thinking about it makes me feel nauseous.

Sorrow wraps itself around me. It is not an emotion that ever pricks you like a needle would. It is an emotion that comes on so gradually that you do not notice until it finally overwhelms you.

As we stood in the check-in line, I thought and thought. Why were these emotions fighting me? We were slowly moving up in line, but my thoughts were getting more and more jumbled. I looked up. We were at the counter. The man's chubby face jolted me. I knew why!

These emotions weren't really fighting me. These emotions were fighting each other. They were all pushing each other around. Whichever emotion went deepest in one's heart won. It was like a game, yet it wasn't.

We were sitting in the waiting room now.

I realized that this trip had not only taught me about China and its way of life but it had also taught me a lot about myself. My biggest discovery was that no matter what, emotions followed you everywhere. Nothing could stop them from coming and nothing could stop them from leaving.

When I had just started out on this trip, I had all these emotions. I had felt sorry for myself and I had thought that would be the most conflicting moment of my life. I never knew that everything in life conflicted so.

I never thought that coming back to the U.S. would cause such a stir in my heart. I thought I would want desperately to come home. I thought I would be incredibly excited about coming back. Just thinking about my earlier predictions made me want to laugh.

The plane was slowly taxiing around the field. I remembered our goodbye to Helen. That seemed to be the only thing that I had done that wasn't robotic. I almost burst out crying.

The plane went faster and faster. My thoughts swirled around me. I felt a jolt. We were slowly climbing into the air.

Slowly, my thoughts organized themselves.

I was leaving. There was no question about that. Only one thought was completely clear and free from everything else:

I would be coming back!